FUNDAMENTALS
OF
MOTOR
BEHAVIOR

FUNDAMENTALS
OF
MOTOR
BEHAVIOR

*Human Kinetics' Fundamentals of
Sport and Exercise Science Series*

Jeffrey T. Fairbrother, PhD

University of Tennessee, Knoxville

HUMAN KINETICS

Library of Congress Cataloging-In-Publication Data

Fairbrother, Jeffrey T., 1964-
  Fundamentals of motor behavior / Jeffrey T. Fairbrother.
    p. cm. -- (Human Kinetics' fundamentals of sport and exercise science series)
  Includes bibliographical references and index.
  ISBN-13: 978-0-7360-7714-9 (soft cover)
  ISBN-10: 0-7360-7714-6 (soft cover)
  1. Motor learning--Textbooks. I. Title.
  BF295.F35 2010
  612.7'6--dc22

                              2009039395

ISBN-10: 0-7360-7714-6 (print)
ISBN-13: 978-0-7360-7714-9 (print)

The Web addresses cited in this text were current as of September 2009, unless otherwise noted.

Acquisitions Editor: Judy Patterson Wright, PhD; **Developmental Editor:** Christine M. Drews; **Assistant Editors:** Dena P. Mumm and Melissa J. Zavala; **Copyeditor:** Joyce Sexton; **Proofreader:** Joanna Hatzopoulos Portman; **Indexer:** Betty Frizzell; **Permission Manager:** Dalene Reeder; **Graphic Designer:** Bob Reuther; **Graphic Artist:** Kim McFarland; **Cover Designer:** Bob Reuther; **Photographer (interior):** © Human Kinetics, unless otherwise noted; **Photo Asset Manager:** Laura Fitch; **Visual Production Assistant:** Joyce Brumfield; **Photo Production Manager:** Jason Allen; **Art Manager:** Kelly Hendren; **Associate Art Manager:** Alan L. Wilborn; **Illustrator:** TwoJay!; **Printer:** Versa Press

Printed in the United States of America   10   9   8   7   6   5   4   3   2   1

The paper in this book is certified under a sustainable forestry program.

Human Kinetics
Web site: www.HumanKinetics.com

United States: Human Kinetics
P.O. Box 5076
Champaign, IL 61825-5076
800-747-4457
e-mail: humank@hkusa.com

Canada: Human Kinetics
475 Devonshire Road Unit 100
Windsor, ON N8Y 2L5
800-465-7301 (in Canada only)
e-mail: info@hkcanada.com

Europe: Human Kinetics
107 Bradford Road
Stanningley
Leeds LS28 6AT, United Kingdom
+44 (0) 113 255 5665
e-mail: hk@hkeurope.com

Australia: Human Kinetics
57A Price Avenue
Lower Mitcham, South Australia 5062
08 8372 0999
e-mail: info@hkaustralia.com

New Zealand: Human Kinetics
P.O. Box 80
Torrens Park, South Australia 5062
0800 222 062
e-mail: info@hknewzealand.com

E4635

To Jenna, for the wonder and joy
you have brought to my life

Contents

Series Preface

The sport sciences have matured impressively over the past 40 years. Subdisciplines in kinesiology have established their own rigorous paths of research, and physical education in its many forms is now an accepted discipline in higher education. Our need now is not only for comprehensive resources that contain all the knowledge that the field has acquired, but also for resources that summarize the foundations of each of the sport sciences for the variety of people who make use of that information today. Understanding the basic topics, goals, and applications of the subdisciplines in kinesiology is critical for students and professionals in many walks of life. Human Kinetics has developed the Fundamentals of Sport and Exercise Science series with these needs in mind.

This and the other books in the series will not provide you with all the in-depth knowledge required for earning an advanced degree or for opening a practice in this subject area. This book will not make you an expert on the subject. What this book will do is give you an excellent grounding in the key themes, terms, history, and status of the subject in both the academic and professional worlds. You can use this grounding as a jumping-off point for studying more in-depth resources and for generating questions for more experienced people in the field. We've even included an annotated list of additional resources for you to consult as you continue your journey.

You might be using this book to help you improve your professional skills or to assess the potential job market. You might want to learn about a new subject, supplement a textbook, or introduce a colleague or client to this exciting subject area. In any of these cases, this book will be your guide to the basics of this subject. It is succinct,

Key to Icons

  Look for the giant quotation marks, which set off noteworthy quotes from researchers and professionals in the field.

 Skill Insights include quirky or surprising "Did you know?" types of information.

Technology Highlights show how researchers and professionals are using technology to analyze movement and advance the field.

 Success Stories highlight influential individuals in the field. Through these sidebars, you will learn how researchers and professionals apply their knowledge of the subject to their work, and you'll be able to explore possible career paths in the field.

informative, and entertaining. You will begin the book with many questions, and you will surely finish it with many more questions. But they will be more thoughtful, complex, substantive questions. We hope that you will use this book to help the sport sciences, and this subject in particular, continue to prosper for another generation.

Preface

There are few observable human behaviors that do not involve some sort of movement. Accordingly, the study of human movement is an important part of our efforts to understand human behavior in general. In addition, movement is a fundamental part of our lives. We use movement to negotiate our way through each day, completing various activities of daily living such as brushing our teeth, opening a can of food, or bathing ourselves. We also use movement to help us perform at work. Even the most sedentary jobs require a vast number of motor skills such as typing, writing, or dialing a telephone. Some jobs, such as those held by professional athletes, are almost entirely based on movement skills.

We also use movement to enhance our health and the quality and enjoyment of our lives. The benefits of regular exercise are well established, but we also use movement when we participate in a wide range of recreational activities such as art (e.g., painting, drawing, or pottery), music, recreational sport, or hobbies (e.g., model building or woodworking). In fact, movement is so central to our lives that most of us enjoy watching others engage in various forms of movement or appreciate the outcome of those movements (e.g., dance, music, art, or sport).

The purpose of this book is to provide an overview of the field of motor behavior. Although it includes many of the same topics you will find in more traditional textbooks, it differs from them in a couple of important ways. First, this book is written so that you do not need specialized knowledge to understand the concepts presented, and the material frequently focuses on why the information is relevant in the real world. Second, the book is organized in a way that first introduces the field and then provides some ideas about what you might be able to do with the knowledge you will gain by entering the field. The "what you can do" part is addressed in chapter 2 as I look at potential career options such as coach, physical educator, or university professor, and throughout the book as I present information about the types of activities you will be able to engage in such as performance analysis and instructional design.

This book is divided into two major sections, the first of which welcomes you to the field of motor behavior. In chapter 1, you will learn what the field of motor behavior is, how it emerged, what questions interest people in the field, and how they go about trying to answer these questions. In chapter 2, you will learn about some of the career paths that relate to motor behavior, and you will be shown some practical examples of how knowledge from the field can be applied in a variety of performance settings.

eBook
available at
HumanKinetics.com

The second section of the book will introduce you to some of the topics that are actually studied in the field of motor behavior. The goal in this section is to introduce you to topics of interest, show you how they are examined, and demonstrate how the knowledge resulting from these examinations can be applied to improve performance in a variety of settings. In chapter 3, you will learn about some of the techniques that practitioners use to observe behavior, as well as the systems for classifying motor behavior in order to identify performance demands. In chapter 4, you will learn about how people control movements. Some movements are slow enough to allow the performer to make adjustments during the action while others are so rapid that they must be entirely planned in advance. Of course, many actions have aspects of both types of movements. Starting a car's ignition provides a good example of such a combined action. The initial movement to turn the key is rapid and probably planned in advance, but the portion during which you hold the key in the "on" position is performed more slowly as you wait for the sound of the ignition.

In chapter 5, you will read about how people learn motor skills. Topics include learning without actual awareness of the learning (i.e., implicit learning), mental practice, learning through observation of others, and the ways in which the type and amount of feedback influence learning. In chapter 6, you will learn about the capabilities and limitations that humans possess with respect to meeting certain task demands. In many situations, the amount of time needed to react to an event is much greater than the length of the event itself. For example, a jab in boxing probably takes about 50 milliseconds to execute, but it takes over 100 milliseconds to process the information that tells you the jab is taking place. The seeming limitation is countered by the ability to anticipate upcoming events. Without the capability to anticipate, a boxing match would not be possible.

In chapter 7, you will learn about some of the considerations involved in establishing procedures for scheduling the practice of multiple tasks to most benefit learning. In chapter 8, you will learn about the motor skill learning cycle, which guides practitioners through the general steps of developing (and revising when needed) a sound instructional approach. Key aspects of the cycle include the development of goals, instructions, target behaviors, and the corresponding measures and feedback.

In an effort to maintain a conversational tone throughout this book, I wrote it as if I were simply sharing with you my understanding of motor behavior. Although this approach was effective, it also presented a challenge when it came to giving credit to the works on which my understanding is based. I have made every effort to indicate the sources for my ideas with reference citations throughout the text. In some cases, the ideas came directly from the cited work. In other cases, the references were included because they had clearly influenced my thinking on a certain topic or served as good examples from the research literature.

My understanding of motor behavior has obviously been influenced by the books and articles that I have read. The two books that have most influenced my thinking have been Schmidt and Wrisberg's *Motor Performance and Learning* and Schmidt and Lee's *Motor Control and Learning*. At the end of the book I have also included a bibliography of readings that have contributed to my own education in the field of motor behavior.

The book closes, in the epilogue, with a discussion about the future of the field of motor behavior. You will learn about some of the unresolved questions relating to how people control their movements and learn motor skills, as well as about how the results of research can best be applied to practical settings. Finally, you will be asked to consider the ways in which your interests in motor behavior might lead you to contribute to the evolution of the field. Motor behavior is a fascinating field because it focuses on something so central to all of our lives—movement. I hope this book helps you understand the principles of motor behavior and how they apply to a variety of professions (and our everyday lives). I wish you the best as you continue your study of this exciting aspect of human behavior.

Acknowledgments

I want to thank several people for their contributions as I wrote this book. Craig A. Wrisberg first recommended me to the publisher as a potential author. His advice, ideas, and feedback influenced much of the material in this book. Craig has been a generous colleague, mentor, and friend. Acquisitions editor Judy Wright and developmental editor Chris Drews did an outstanding job of patiently guiding me through the unfamiliar territory of book publishing. Other people who helped me better understand the performance demands of certain sports and movement activities included Joao Barros (swimming), Greg Young (soccer), and Duncan Simpson (tennis).

Finally, I offer my deep gratitude to my wife, Julie Fairbrother, for her unwavering support and encouragement, and for keeping me focused as I neared the finish line.

I

PART

Welcome to Motor Behavior

In the first part of this book, two preliminary questions about the field of motor behavior are asked and answered. Chapter 1 answers the question "What is motor behavior?" by briefly describing some of the issues and problems that interest people in the field. In addition, a short history of motor behavior is presented to illustrate the origin of the field and the way in which it relates to other disciplines interested in human performance and learning. The first chapter closes with a description of some of the fields that are closely related to motor behavior, such as sport psychology, physical education, occupational therapy, and human factors.

Chapter 2 answers the question "What can I do with motor behavior?" in two distinct ways. First, the chapter relates some examples of how the concepts and principles of motor behavior can be used to address performance and learning issues in the real world. Second, you will learn about the various career paths that involve an understanding of motor behavior, including the academic path, several professional paths, and some other creative career paths that are probably not as easy to recognize.

Chapters 1 and 2 include the first of the technology highlights that are a recurring feature throughout the book. The technology highlights describe how professionals in fields relying on motor behavior use technology to better understand and, when possible, facilitate motor performance and learning. Technology highlights include topics like video analysis, simulator training, computerized testing software, eye tracking, and various other training and measurement devices.

CHAPTER 1

What Is Motor Behavior?

© Stephen Blose/Fotolia.com

In this chapter you will learn the following:

✓ What the three subdisciplines within the field of motor behavior are
✓ How the field of motor behavior developed historically
✓ About several professional fields that use the principles of motor behavior

> Champions
> keep playing until
> they get it right.
>
> **Billie Jean King**

Imagine that you are asked to determine which individuals out of an extremely large group are most likely to succeed at a given task. Imagine also that the success of your selection process has great importance not only to you and the people you are evaluating, but also to the entire population of the country in which you live. How would you go about making your decisions? This is the scenario that military officials in the United States faced in selecting and training pilots during World War II. During the first two years of involvement, approximately 400,000 men applied to become pilots through the Aviation Cadet Program. To test such large numbers, selection procedures needed to be readily available and relatively inexpensive. The success of the selection process depended upon identifying who was likely to succeed and who was likely to fail during training. Being too strict during selection would not produce enough pilots to meet the growing demand caused by the war. On the other hand, a less stringent selection process would waste limited resources and risk lives. What types of tests would you use to predict whether someone would be a good pilot? Ultimately, the military used a battery of intelligence, personality, and perceptual-motor skills tests. Of the candidates selected, about 75 percent made it through the first stage of training,

Principles of motor performance were used to select pilots during World War II.

about 65 percent made it through the second stage, and about 62 percent received their "wings" (Ashcroft, 2005; Wells, 1997).

motor behavior—A field of study devoted to understanding how humans control their movements and learn movement skills.

motor performance—Observable behavior that can be taken as a measure of a person's capability to complete a motor skill.

■   ■   ■

Motor behavior is a field devoted to understanding how humans control their movements and learn movement skills. Some researchers also focus on the movements of animals, but this book will deal primarily with human behaviors. Often, the term *motor behavior* is used to refer broadly to the field or to various activities that involve movement. When we observe people to assess their movements, we use the term **motor performance** to refer to what we can see and measure. For example, a physical therapist might observe a patient's motor performance in executing an exercise designed to strengthen the muscles that support the shoulder. In observing this motor performance, the therapist might note the amount of weight used, the number of repetitions completed, and the quality of the movement (i.e., whether or not the technique or skill was correctly executed).

There are two general categories of professional activity within the field of motor behavior, both of which are concerned with gathering information about movements: research and practical application.

Research

Research in motor behavior is conducted in several steps. First, the researcher identifies a question or problem to be addressed. For example, how does the complexity of a movement influence the amount of time it takes to prepare that movement? This preparation time is called *reaction time,* and it represents the amount of time that passes between the signal to start and the beginning of movement. Second, the researcher identifies the different factors that might be expected to influence a motor skill. In the example just mentioned, the researcher thinks that movement complexity is a factor that might influence reaction time. Third, the researcher will try to control or measure (or both) all of the factors that might influence the motor skill. The means of controlling movement complexity would probably involve having the participants perform simple, intermediate, and complex versions of a skill. Reaction time would then be measured for each of these versions. The final step of the research process is to compare the different conditions, which in this case would mean comparing the reaction times for each of the three skill variations (simple, intermediate, and complex) to see if the more complex versions required longer reaction times.

In a well-known study, Henry and Rogers (1960) investigated the problem I just described by examining how the complexity and duration of an arm movement influenced the amount of time it took participants to *prepare* to move. Their results showed that it takes more time to prepare for a more complex movement than it does for a less complex movement. This finding is particularly important if the speed at which someone responds to a cue is an important part of the performance.

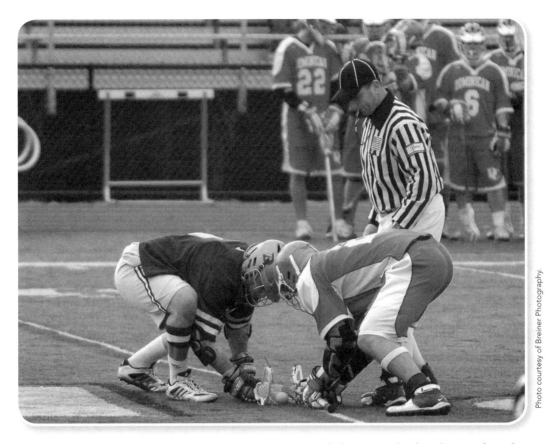

Photo courtesy of Breiner Photography.

FIGURE 1.1 The time it takes athletes to *prepare* to move is important in situations such as the face-off in lacrosse.

For example, in the sport of lacrosse, two players sometimes engage in a face-off (see figure 1.1). During a face-off, the ball is placed on the ground between the two players, who each line up in a four-point stance (i.e., both feet and both hands are on the ground supporting weight) with their sticks on the ground. When the official signals, the two players move as quickly as possible to gain possession of the ball. Several different moves are involved in capturing the ball, each requiring an extremely rapid response. In addition to trying to get the ball into the net on the stick, the players will use their bodies and their sticks to interfere with each other. The complexity of the response is an important consideration in a face-off because any advantage you gain by using a sophisticated technique may be offset by the extra preparation time required before you even begin to execute it.

Practical Application

The other category of professional activity within the field of motor behavior involves the practical application of concepts and principles to facilitate performance and learning. People who focus on this aspect of motor behavior are often called *practitioners*. You are probably familiar with some of the more widely known types of movement practitioners such as coaches, physical educators, and physical therapists, but practitioners in many other occupations also regularly consider ways of improving movement performance and learning. These include trainers in commercial, industrial, and military settings; dance, music, and art instructors; occupational and speech therapists; and voice coaches. Indeed, because movement is so central to our existence, the practical application of principles and concepts from motor behavior can benefit nearly every aspect of life.

It is important to remember that research and practical application are not mutually exclusive. Many researchers are also interested in practical application, and many practitioners are involved in conducting research. It is best to think of research and application as two types of professional activities rather than two different types of professions. Although a coach might not publish research articles in scholarly journals, her long-term success will often depend upon the depth of understanding of her sport that she has developed through systematic observation. To return to the lacrosse example, an experienced coach who has observed many face-offs involving players of different skill levels would probably recognize that although players might experience low success when first using a sophisticated technique, they will be able to overcome this drawback after extensive practice. In other words, a highly complex but thoroughly practiced response can sometimes be quicker than a less complex but less practiced response.

Skill Insight

Expert coaches use the principles of motor behavior to prepare their athletes. A study of the coaching behaviors of basketball coach Jerry Tarkanian (Bloom, Crumpton, & Anderson, 1999) revealed that the majority of his statements during practice were consistent with the effective principles of instruction that have emerged from motor behavior research. For example, about 43 percent of his statements focused on instruction related to skills or tactics to execute those skills.

Three Subdisciplines

The field of motor behavior is commonly divided into three subdisciplines called **motor control, motor development,** and **motor learning.**

Motor Control

In general, professionals interested in motor control tend to focus on topics related to how we control our movements. They often attempt to explain the control of movements in terms of how the brain and central nervous system interact with muscles. In addition, mechanical factors such as muscle forces and limb velocities are often incorporated into their explanations. These professionals might be interested in how we coordinate two

motor control—A subdiscipline within the field of motor behavior that is concerned with neurological, mechanical, and behavioral explanations of how humans control movements.

or more of our limbs during the execution of a complex task. We see a real-world example of this in an overhand tennis serve in which the player must precisely coordinate the movements of the ball-tossing arm with the swinging motion of the racket arm. Advanced players jump into the air during this motion, so the overall action also requires coordination of the jump with the movements of the arms. Another example is seen when a person plays a piece of music on a piano, which requires the simultaneous control of both hands and feet. Professionals in motor control are also interested in other topics such as how we use vision to guide reaching actions and how people control their posture.

Motor Development

Professionals interested in motor development tend to focus on topics pertaining to changes in motor performance associated with development during childhood, changes associated with aging during adulthood, and factors that influence normal development. For example, these professionals might be interested in how children learn to walk or how our capability to balance degrades as we age. Many people unfamiliar with motor development mistakenly believe that it focuses only on children's learning of basic movement skills such as jumping, hopping, and throwing. In reality, the focus is on what is often called life span motor development. This means that while some professionals may be mostly interested in how children learn to crawl, others might be more interested in addressing how older adults relearn to walk after a knee or hip replacement.

motor development—A subdiscipline of the field of motor behavior concerned with changes in motor performance that occur as people move through different phases of the life span (e.g., childhood development and aging).

Motor Learning

Professionals interested in motor learning tend to focus on how we learn to perform skilled movements such as those involved in sport, work settings, or everyday activities. For example, these professionals might be interested in how different practice schedules (e.g., practicing one task at a time compared to practicing several tasks together) contribute to learning baseball pitches, how virtual reality or simulations can be used to train pilots and surgeons, or how the administration of feedback affects learning to drive a car.

Learning is not something that can be observed directly, so we draw conclusions about how much a person has learned by examining the person's motor performance at different times. During practice, we expect performance to improve, but we can conclude that people have learned a motor skill if they can perform it even after they have not practiced for some time. Sports offer a good example. We can observe a person's motor performance of a basketball free throw during both practice and games, but we might see fairly different results in these two situations. During practice, performance might be improved by instruction and feedback from the coach, or it might be degraded by the fact that several players are shooting at the goal at the same time. The presence

motor learning—A subdiscipline of the field of motor behavior that is interested in explanations of how people learn motor skills; a set of internal processes that produce relatively permanent improvements in a person's capability to effectively complete a motor skill.

of temporary influences such as these tells us that performance during practice is not a reflection of motor learning. The game, however, can be thought of as a test of learning. If a basketball player shoots well in a game, we can conclude that he has learned something from the activities he completed during practice. An even stronger indication is if the player continues to shoot well, because this suggests that the skill is stable (i.e., well learned).

The test of an outfielder's skill comes when he has to go against the fence to make a catch.

Joe DiMaggio

Topics of Interest to All Three Subdisciplines

Many professionals are involved in work that would fall under more than one of the three subdisciplines. For example, several researchers have examined the effects of different practice schedules (e.g., a random presentation of three skills vs. a blocked presentation in which each skill is practiced separately) on motor learning in adults and children. While the topic of practice schedule effects is typically thought of as a *motor learning* topic, the ways in which these effects may differ between children and adults could also be thought of as a *motor development* topic. As with the distinction between research and application, it is probably best not to think of the three subdisciplines as exclusive professional niches. Instead, I recommend that you think of these subdisciplines as useful reminders of the variety of interests that can be pursued within the field of motor behavior. While in practice it may be true that individuals tend to have a primary focus in their professional lives (e.g., working with children or in rehabilitation settings), issues related to motor behavior can often defy simple categorization because movement occurs in so many aspects of our lives.

One topic of interest that cuts across the three subdisciplines relates to how we can improve the ways in which we help people suffering from a handicapping condition (e.g., stroke, cerebral palsy, or Parkinson's disease). While diseases like cerebral palsy and Parkinson's may affect only children and adults, respectively, most people would acknowledge that understanding how a person copes with the debilitating effects of one condition can potentially be used to help people suffering from another condition. In terms of movement, these conditions share a common feature in that an affected individual must meet specific movement demands within everyday contexts.

Skill Insight

Common advice to keep the head still while putting a golf ball seems to be incorrect. Tim Lee and colleagues (2008) looked at the head movements of skilled and unskilled golfers and found that both groups moved their heads. The difference was that the skilled golfers moved their heads in the direction opposite that of their swing—probably so that the two movements offset one another—while unskilled golfers moved their heads in the same direction as their swing.

ORGANIZATIONS FOR MOTOR BEHAVIOR

The following list includes professional organizations that sponsor conferences at which motor behavior research is presented. The organizations are appropriate for academic motor behavior researchers.

North America

American Alliance for Health, Physical Education, Recreation and Dance   www.aahperd.org

American College of Sports Medicine   www.acsm.org

American Psychological Association, Division 47   www.apa47.org

Canadian Society for Psychomotor Learning and Sport Psychology   www.scapps.org

Gait and Clinical Movement Analysis Society   www.gcmas.org

Human Factors and Ergonomics Society   www.hfes.org

National Association of Kinesiology and Physical Education in Higher Education
   www.nakpehe.org

North American Society for the Psychology of Sport and Physical Activity   www.naspspa.org

Society for Neuroscience   www.sfn.org

Europe

British Neuroscience Association   www.bna.org.uk

European College of Sport Sciences   www.ecss.de

European Society of Movement Analysis in Adults and Children   www.esmac2009london.org

German Association of Sport Psychology   www.ispw.unibe.ch/asp/english/index.html

International Association of Sport Kinetics   www.sportkinetics.org

The following list includes professional organizations for fields that frequently rely on the principles of motor behavior. Although motor behavior research might be presented at their conferences, it would not be a central focus. These organizations are appropriate for professionals in the related disciplines.

United States

American Physical Therapy Association   www.apta.org

American Occupational Therapy Association   www.aota.org

Europe

European College of Sports Medicine and Exercise Physicians   www.ecosep.eu

European Physical Education Association   www.eupea.com

Federation of European Ergonomics Societies   www.fees-network.org

The Ergonomics Society   www.ergonomics.org.uk

World Confederation for Physical Therapy   www.wcpt.org

Council of Occupational Therapists for European Countries   www.cotec-europe.org

Asia and Australia

Asia-Pacific Physical Therapy Student Association   www.pt.ntu.edu.tw/apptsa

Australian Council for Health, Physical Education and Recreation   www.achper.org.au

Ergonomics Society of Korea   http://esk.or.kr

Human Factors & Ergonomics Society of Australia   www.ergonomics.org.au

Hong Kong Ergonomics Society   www.ergonomics.org.hk

By understanding the demands faced by those with selected movement disorders, professionals can begin to develop more general treatments that might benefit people with a wider range of conditions affecting movement. Recent research suggests that victims of stroke and individuals with Parkinson's disease can benefit from instructions that direct their attention to the result of the movement rather than to their efforts to control the movement itself (Wulf, 2007b). For example, stroke patients moved a coffee cup faster when they focused on where to place the cup rather than on how to hold their hand and arm during the task.

 Practice is generally considered to be the single most important factor responsible for the permanent improvement in the ability to perform a motor skill.

Mark Guadagnoli and Tim Lee (2004)

Another topic of general interest in the field of motor behavior involves the study of expert performance. Researchers examine the development of expertise by noting how performance improves as a result of learning and maturation. For example, expertise in youth sport is examined without concern for the fact that these athletes are not "experts," in the sense that they are not among the best in the world in their sport.

Examination of expertise in youth sport plays an important role in determining the stages at which experts develop the skills and knowledge that support their superior performance. For example, it is clear that an outstanding tennis player like Roger Federer possesses both the physical skills and the tactical knowledge to be extremely successful in his sport. At this time, however, it is still unknown how these two components might interact during their development. For example, we might ask if it is always useful to acquire advanced tactical knowledge or if a certain level of physical skill must first be reached for such knowledge to provide an advantage. We can start to address these questions by examining the performance and knowledge of high-level youth tennis players.

The study of expert performance is, of course, also concerned with identifying the characteristics that best capture what it means to be an expert in various movement-related endeavors such as surgery, sport, or dance. We know, for example, that anticipation skills differ between expert and nonexpert soccer players (Williams, 2000). When expert and nonexpert soccer players are shown a video of an oncoming player with the ball and the video is stopped before the ball is kicked, expert soccer players are typically more accurate

1880s-1890s

Research Topics
- The use of vision in hand movements
- Photographic analysis of animal locomotion
- The detection of movement sensations
- Sending and receiving skills of telegraph operators

1885 Founding of the Association for the Advancement of Physical Education

1887 Muybridge's *Animal Locomotion*

1894 *Psychological Review* established

1895 Report in *The New York Times* on the invention of a device for measuring the reaction time of runners

1900s-1910s

Research Topics
- The relationship between arousal and performance
- The accuracy of movements
- The discrimination of different weights
- Typewriting skill
- Finger tapping
- The effects of spacing practice sessions

1909 *The British Journal of Psychology* established

1916 *The Journal of Experimental Psychology* established

1920s-1930s

Research Topics
- The effects of knowledge of results (or feedback) on performance
- A clinical perspective of motor learning
- The relationship between stature and physical performance
- Kinesthesis in piano playing
- Learning to drive a golf ball
- Motor ability
- Stages of overhand throwing in children

1926 The American Academy of Kinesiology and Physical Education established

1927 Thorndike's *law of effect* (large impact on motor behavior research)

1930 *The Research Quarterly of the American Physical Education Association* established (often called *The Research Quarterly* or *Research Quarterly*)

1939 Beginning of World War II (need for selection and training of pilots dramatically increases motor behavior research in Great Britain)

than nonexperts in predicting the direction in which the ball will be kicked. In addition, stopping the video at earlier points in the unfolding sequence of events does not seem to hinder the experts as much as it does the nonexperts. In other words, the experts have developed a knowledge base that lets them predict what will happen before it does, which clearly gives them a performance advantage over their nonexpert counterparts.

A Brief History of Motor Behavior

It is probably safe to assume that people have always been intrigued by how we control our movements and learn motor skills. One example of this interest can be found in the Greek myth of Arachne (see figure 1.2; Ovid, ca. 8 AD), who was so skilled at weaving that many people came to watch her work. She even caught the attention of the goddess Athena, who disguised herself and provoked Arachne to begin bragging that she could beat the goddess in a competition. Athena revealed herself and the competition began. There was some debate about who actually won, and at the end of the competition Arachne became distraught with shame at having offended Athena. Just as Arachne was about to hang herself, Athena intervened and

Reprinted from http://en.wikipedia.org/wiki/File:Diego_Vel%C3%A1zquez_014.jpg

FIGURE 1.2 A painting depicting Arachne weaving. The story illustrates an early fascination with movement skills.

turned her into a spider. Thus, spiders are called *arachnids* because of their mastery of weaving. The story of Arachne illustrates the Greeks' interest in skilled movements in two ways. First, the story relates that people were interested enough in Arachne's skill to actually come watch her weave. Second, the story itself is a direct use of the idea of skilled human behavior as a way to understand the natural world.

The modern origins of motor behavior can be traced to research in experimental psychology that was conducted near the end of the 19th century. The first issue of the research journal *Psychological Review* (published in 1894) included a report comparing how well blind and sighted individuals could detect movement sensations in the hand (Delbarre, 1894). Other early studies included photographic analyses of human movement (Muybridge, 1887), examinations of the sending and receiving skills of telegraph operators (Bryan & Harter, 1897), and an investigation of the relationship between movement speed and accuracy (Woodworth, 1899). It is important to note that although much of the research in motor behavior during this period originated from the United States and England, important contributions were also made by scholars from countries such as Germany and France.

During the early part of the 20th century, researchers continued to study movement, focusing on a variety of tasks and topics. Studies were conducted to examine performance on tasks such as typewriting, line drawing, arm movements, finger tapping, driving a golf ball, and throwing. Topics of interest during this period included the relationship between arousal and performance, the spacing of practice attempts, motor abilities, transfer of training, the effects of feedback, and the application of learning theory to industrial and clinical settings.

During World War II, a great deal of research energy was directed toward topics that might help the military select and train pilots. This intense effort was important for the study of motor behavior, and in many ways it marked the emergence of motor behavior as a distinct field of study. When the war ended, research in motor behavior grew tremendously, largely as a result of generous funding provided by the U.S. Air Force or the British Royal Air Force. From that point until the present, the range of topics has expanded dramatically. Two important theoretical perspectives have fueled much of this work. According to the first perspective, movement depends upon the processing of information. This is called the **information processing perspective.** The idea that the brain is similar to a computer gained considerable ground during the immediate postwar period. With the so-called cognitive revolution in the 1960s, researchers began to focus on the mental and neural processes that are thought to underlie movements rather than on just the cause-and-effect relationships between the variables that influence movement and the behaviors they produce.

1940s-1950s

Research Topics
- Motor performance in adolescence
- Movement analysis in industrial training
- The visual movements in professional baseball batters
- Speed–accuracy trade-offs in movement
- The effects of the number of response choices on reaction time
- Psychomotor selection tests for service personnel
- The effects on performance of withdrawing knowledge of results

1941 Entry of the United States into World War II (dramatic increase in motor behavior research in the United States)

1943 Hull's *Principles of Behavior* (large impact on motor learning research)

1947 *The Canadian Journal of Psychology* established

1948 Craik's analogy of the human brain as a computer

1949 The journal *Perceptual and Motor Skills* established

1952 Guthrie's *The Psychology of Learning*

1955 The Australian Council for Health, Physical Education and Recreation established

1956 Miller's paper on the limits of working memory

1959 Crossman's theory on the acquisition of speed skill

1959 Easterbrook's hypothesis of how arousal reduces attentional capacity

1960s-1970s

Research Topics
- Knowledge of results
- Perceptual narrowing in novice drivers
- Learning without sensory feedback
- Motor short-term memory
- The benefits of random practice for motor learning
- The application of motor learning and control research to children

1960 Henry and Roger's memory-drum theory of motor behavior

1964 First motor learning textbook published

1965 Beginning of the first generation of doctoral graduates specializing in the field of motor behavior

1967 Espenchade and Eckert's *Motor Development*
(continued)

information processing perspective—An approach to the study of motor behavior that assumes that people use information from the environment when planning, controlling, and learning movements.

dynamic systems perspective—An approach to the study of motor behavior that assumes that the performer is a part of a larger system; this larger system involves the unique requirements of the task as well as environment-imposed limitations on movements.

According to the second perspective, the performer is just one component of a dynamic system that also involves the task and the environment in which it is performed. This perspective tends to focus on patterns of movement and how they emerge in certain situations. This perspective is called the **dynamic systems perspective.** It grew out of work that the Russian scientist Nicolai Bernstein completed during the 1930s to 1960s. Bernstein's influence expanded dramatically with the first publication of his work in English in the 1960s (Bernstein, 1967).

Today, there continues to be strong international research interest in topics related to the information processing and dynamic systems perspectives. In addition, there has been an increased interest in sport and other applied skills.

 ## SUCCESS STORY

John Shea, Indiana University Ergonomics Laboratory

John Shea, PhD, began his college education at Springfield College in Massachusetts, a pioneering school in the study of physical education. While at Springfield, John earned both a bachelor's and a master's degree and competed on the swim team. He continued his graduate studies at the University of Michigan, where he earned another master's degree and a doctoral degree with a specialization in motor behavior. Since receiving his degree, John has been on the faculty at New York University, the University of Colorado, Penn State University, Florida State University, and Indiana University. During his career, he has achieved a great deal of success as both a researcher (having coauthored one of the more widely cited articles in the field of motor behavior) and an administrator (having served as both a department head and an associate dean for a college).

Photo courtesy of John Shea.

John's research has focused largely on identifying the various factors that influence memory for skilled movements. In one study he showed that memory for movements was enhanced when learners were provided with descriptive labels for the movements (i.e., the hours on the clock to represent the position of a lever to be moved). In another study, he and a colleague demonstrated that practicing three tasks in a random order resulted in better learning than practicing one task completely before moving on to the next. Currently, John is a professor at Indiana University, where he developed and now directs the Ergonomics Laboratory and its associated academic program. John also serves as a consultant for CSX Corporation on matters related to performance and workplace wellness.

For example, the Australian Institute of Sport has a Skill Acquisition staff that conducts research and develops practical applications to help improve the motor skills of the athletes on Australia's national teams. Other topics recently studied by professionals in the field of motor behavior include the relationship between fundamental motor skills (fairly simple motor skills that serve as the building blocks of more complex skills needed in real-world activities) and physical activity levels; balance impairment in children and adults; the role of self-regulation in motor learning; the effects of attentional focus on motor performance and learning; the role of vision in reaching, grasping, and pointing actions; and how multiple limbs can be coupled together in coordinated movements. Of course, the full scope of interest in motor behavior today far exceeds this listing, and in fact is so broad that all the interests would be hard even to list. Because movement is a part of virtually every facet of life, it is likely that there are professionals who are interested in understanding every corresponding aspect of movement. While this makes it difficult to give an encompassing view of the field, it shows the relevance of motor behavior for a wide range of professional activities, and personally I find it exciting that there are so many things to learn about movement.

Related Fields of Study

Because motor behavior encompasses such a broad range of topics, there are many related fields. However, there are a few fields that are traditionally very closely aligned with motor behavior. First among these is the field of *experimental psychology,* especially those aspects that have been concerned with perception, performance, and learning. Indeed, much of the earliest motor behavior research was conducted by experimental psychologists, and there are still many researchers in this field who are actively engaged in studying movement. *Sport psychology* is also a closely related field, as it focuses on many of the same issues pertaining to motor behavior but within the context of sport. Another field that emerged about the same time that motor behavior started to become independent from experimental psychology is known as *human factors* or *ergonomics*. The field of human factors focuses on the interactions between machines and their human operators. There is considerable overlap between human factors and motor behavior.

Physical education and *exercise science* (also known as *kinesiology*) are two more fields that are closely related to motor behavior. In fact, college courses in motor learning, motor control, and motor development have traditionally been taught within physical education and exercise science programs. The fields of *physical*

1960s-1970s
(continued)

- **1967** Bernstein's *The Co-ordination and Regulation of Movements* published in English (originally published in Russian in 1947)
- **1967** The North American Society for the Psychology of Sport and Physical Activity established
- **1969** *The Journal of Motor Behavior* established
- **1971** Adams' closed-loop theory of motor learning
- **1974** Human Kinetics established (the company's first publication is the proceedings of the 1973 meeting of the North American Society for the Psychology of Sport and Physical Activity)
- **1975** Schmidt's schema theory of motor learning
- **1977** The Canadian Society for Psychomotor Learning and Sport Psychology established
- **1979** A paper advocating the dynamical systems perspective published in *Science*

1980s-1990s

Research Topics
- The effects of variability of practice on motor learning
- The control of reaching and grasping
- The effects of various knowledge of results manipulations
- The benefit of allowing a learner to control the administration of feedback
- Observational learning
- Visual search strategies in expert soccer players
- The effects of practice schedules on motor learning

- **1981** The Australian Institute of Sport established
- **1982** The first graduate-level text published
- **1982** Kelso and Clark's *The Development of Movement Control and Co-ordination* (advocates the use of the dynamical systems perspective to study motor development)
- **1986** Haywood's *Life Span Motor Development*
- **1986** Division 47 of the American Psychological Association established
- **1989** Korean Institute of Sport Science founded
- **1991** Rosenbaum's *Human Motor Control*

(continued)

and *occupational therapy* are also closely related to motor behavior. While both forms of therapy focus on treatments to restore functional movement capabilities to individuals who have some type of movement impairment, occupational therapy tends to emphasize functional goal-directed actions. For example, to restore range of motion at the shoulder joint, physical therapy might involve strength training exercises requiring the arm to be lifted above the shoulder, while occupational therapy might involve asking the patient to place cans of food on an overhead shelf.

 TECHNOLOGY HIGHLIGHT

Eadweard Muybridge's Photographic Analyses

Eadweard Muybridge was an English photographer who developed a method of using multiple cameras to capture the motion of moving animals (including humans). One of his most famous contributions to the understanding of movement came about when he provided photographic evidence to determine if all four hooves left the ground at the same time when a horse galloped (Clegg, 2007). As you can see from the figure, Muybridge's work showed that the horse did indeed have all four of its hooves off the ground at certain points during the gallop (second and third frames of top row). Muybridge's technique was a precursor to film- and video-based analyses, as well as the more sophisticated motion capture systems used today. Note that although these photographs were intended to provide information about horse galloping, a careful examination also reveals information about how the rider regulated his position in the saddle depending on the phase of the gallop.

Photo courtesy of Library of Congress. LC-USZ62-45683

The Short of It

- Motor behavior is a term that refers to both a field of research and a broad range of movement activities. The principles that have emerged from research in motor behavior apply to a wide range of professions that focus on movement (e.g., rehabilitation, coaching, and physical education).

- There are three subdisciplines within the field of motor behavior. Motor control focuses on issues related to how people control their movements. Motor development focuses on motor performance changes across the life span. Motor learning focuses on motor performance changes that result from different practice conditions. All three subdisciplines are interested in the study of movement disorders and the development of movement expertise.

- The field of motor behavior emerged from experimental psychology in large part due to efforts to efficiently select and train pilots during World War II. Today, motor behavior is related to a wide variety of fields that also involve the study of human performance. These include human factors, occupational therapy, physical education, coaching, exercise science, and physical therapy.

CHAPTER 2

What Can I Do With Motor Behavior?

STEPHANE KEMPINAIRE/DPPI/Icon SMI

✓ The preparation required for an academic position in the field of motor behavior and some of the typical characteristics of such a career

✓ How two of the many different types of professional positions benefit from training in motor behavior

✓ How expertise in motor behavior can be used in a consulting career

The secret to getting ahead is getting started.

Mark Twain

You have just secured a job as a sport technologist with your country's Olympic committee. Your first assignment is to work with swimmers to help them gain any performance advantage they can. Some of your coworkers are testing the performance swimsuits that reportedly reduce friction between the swimmer and the water. Because you are a new hire, your first assignment is to get to know the coaches and learn about how the athletes currently train. After you have observed several practices, one of the coaches points out that swimmers continue to use a staggered push-off when they complete flip turns despite the fact that the coaches have been emphasizing the importance of pushing evenly with both feet. The coach asks you if you have any idea why the swimmers continue to use the staggered push-off. Is it because they have trouble learning the other technique, or have they discovered a better technique? What do you think? How would you go about answering this question? According to Peter Vint, a sport technologist with the U.S. Olympic Committee, the staggered push-off is similar to staggered jumps in other sports such as volleyball and basketball that produce more power (Upton, 2008). So, he thinks the athletes may be correct in their preference for the staggered push-off. He hopes to investigate this in the future by installing a force plate in the wall of a swimming pool to compare the two techniques.

■   ■   ■

In chapter 1, you read about the wide variety of topics that interest professionals in motor behavior and other closely related fields. This chapter provides an overview of selected careers that either depend on or are enhanced by knowledge of motor behavior, and also presents information about the types of training needed to pursue different careers. The first section describes the *academic path,* which typically leads to a college or university position. The second section describes two different *professional paths,* both of which are highly dependent upon an understanding of the principles of motor behavior: physical educator and occupational therapist. The third section deals with what might be called *side paths* to careers as a *human performance consultant* or a *skill acquisition specialist.*

As I noted in chapter 1, the term *motor behavior* refers not only to a professional field, but also to a phenomenon. That is, people *move.* So, the term motor behavior also refers to behavior of people that involves movement as one of its primary components. This, of course, includes virtually all activities in life, and thus the principles of motor behavior apply to a wide variety of professions that focus on human movement of one sort or another. The following are just a few examples of how issues in motor control, development, and learning can apply to a range of professional activities.

- Trainers in industries that use production lines (e.g., aircraft and auto manufacturing) teach employees how to operate machinery in safe and effective ways. Often, this has to do with specific movement techniques such as those involved in the correct way to hold and manipulate a tool.

- Military trainers use a variety of practice activities (e.g., drills and simulations) to teach recruits a range of motor skills, including how to disassemble and reassemble weapons and how to run, climb, and crawl while loaded with gear.

- Trainers in restaurants teach new employees how to balance a tray filled with glasses and how to carry four or more food plates at a time. Both of these skills typically require the trainee to practice specific techniques under the supervision of a trainer who provides feedback and correction.

- Art instructors teach their students how to hold a paintbrush correctly and develop an appropriate stroke technique so that the brush applies the correct amount of paint to the canvas.

Skill Insight

A major component of the Professional Golf Management program offered by the PGA (Professional Golf Association) involves learning how to analyze a golfer's swing and implement effective instruction. This component is delivered in three parts. The first part focuses on the fundamentals of the golf swing and various instructional techniques. The second part focuses on helping the golf professional learn how to effectively communicate with students, assess their swings, and fit them with the appropriate clubs. In addition, the golf professional observes an advanced teaching professional delivering instruction. The third part focuses on the application of the concepts learned in the first two parts. The golf professional is evaluated on his ability to identify swing flaws, teach difficult shot techniques, and use video-based motion analysis systems (PGA of America, 2008).

- Occupational therapists help patients improve a variety of movement skills, often through the completion of what might be called a functional activity. For example, a patient might be asked to set a dinner table—an activity that involves reaching and grasping, fine motor control used in placing silverware, and coordination of the reaching limb with postural adjustments of the trunk. Because therapists typically work with patients ranging from children to older adults, the therapies they use will vary according to the developmental needs of the patient.

- Physical therapists, athletic trainers, and fitness professionals help their patients, athletes, or clients learn to coordinate different body parts to correctly execute strength training exercises.

- Instructors who teach surgical skills help doctors learn correct scalpel technique when making an incision or how to control an instrument that they can see only on a video monitor.

At this point, you probably recognize that the list of possible examples is practically endless. See if you can identify issues related to motor control, development, or learning involved in the activities of these others: dance instructors, music teachers, and skilled carpenters supervising their apprentices.

Academic Path

The academic career path involves extensive education, usually requiring that you obtain the equivalent of a bachelor's degree, a master's degree, and a **doctoral degree** (figure 2.1). Typically, the doctorate includes a specialization in one of the subdisciplines of motor behavior (i.e., motor learning, motor control, or motor development). Remember, however, that other disciplines such as experimental psychology can also lead to academic work in motor behavior. The first step in the educational process is the bachelor's degree. While majors such as kinesiology, exercise science, physical education, or psychology will give you a good start, they are not absolutely required. For example, my undergraduate degree is in English.

doctoral degree—The highest academic degree granted by colleges and universities.

The next step is to obtain a master's degree. At this level, specialization in related majors such as kinesiology becomes more important, but other science majors such as psychology or biology can also give you a good foundation for future work. If you have an unrelated undergraduate degree, it is common practice among many schools

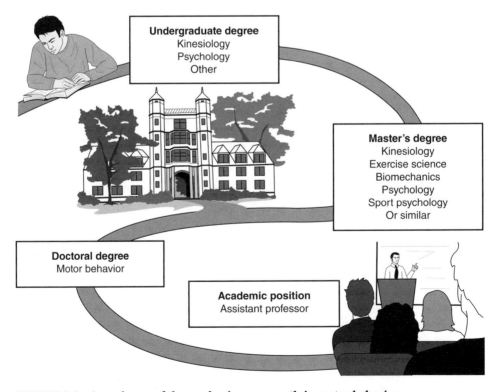

FIGURE 2.1 A road map of the academic career path in motor behavior.

to require you to take additional courses during your master's degree program to ensure that you have an adequate background in the topics you are studying. This seems to be particularly true for science courses. It is important to recognize that having to take additional courses as a graduate student can substantially increase the cost of your education. So, to the extent that you can, it is a good idea to find out the entrance requirements of different master's programs in advance and take as many of the prerequisites as you can as an undergraduate. In preparation for moving on to a doctoral program, it is a good idea to get involved in research during your master's degree program. Some doctoral programs expect students to have completed a master's thesis to demonstrate a basic level of proficiency in the research process.

The greater danger for most of us lies not in setting our aim too high and falling short; but in setting our aim too low, and achieving our mark.

Michelangelo

The final step in your education will be a doctoral program, during which you will likely be involved in a number of research projects. In most cases, you will also be given the opportunity to teach or assist professors with classes. It is important to develop your skills as both a researcher and a teacher, as both of these can be important aspects of academic jobs. It typically takes three to five years to complete a doctoral degree with a specialization in motor behavior. The final year of your doctoral program is your dissertation year, during which you will complete a research study under the guidance of your major professor. After receiving your doctorate, you will try to secure a job either as an assistant professor or in a **postdoctoral position.** Postdoctoral positions typically focus exclusively on research and are often funded by grant money awarded to an institution to support a specific line of research for a given length of time (this is particularly true in the United States). Sometimes universities, government agencies, or charitable foundations award postdoctoral fellowships that are not restricted to a specific project but can be used at eligible institutions to pursue a specific type of research. For example, the University of Western Australia offers fellowships to support work in a specific department selected by the applicant. If you are interested in a career as a researcher, postdoctoral positions can be a great way to establish a track record. In motor behavior, most postdoctoral positions are for research projects related to motor control issues, so opportunities will depend upon your specialization during your doctoral program.

postdoctoral position—A transitional job focusing on research; held by a person who has received a doctoral degree but usually has not yet started a professional career as an academic.

When you are searching for a position as an assistant professor, there are a few important things to keep in mind. Universities and colleges differ in terms of how much they emphasize research and teaching. At institutions that are called research universities, teaching is usually considered an important endeavor, but professors teach fewer classes than at other types of schools. Instead, the focus is on generating published research and acquiring grant money to support research projects.

At other types of schools, the relative importance of teaching and research differs depending upon the mission of the institution. For example, some colleges that focus primarily on undergraduate education require very little in the way of research, but professors may teach as many as four or five classes a semester. In either case, a career as an academic can be very rewarding. One of the benefits is a high degree of independence to pursue the topics you are interested in.

Although not all academic positions are alike, I can give you a good sense of the day-to-day job requirements by describing in general terms the types of things I do in my current position at the University of Tennessee (or UT). The University of Tennessee is considered a research university, so my job entails a good deal of both teaching and research. During a typical week, I will teach one undergraduate course and one graduate course, each meeting for 75 minutes twice a week. So, I spend about 5 hours a week in the classroom. Of course, my teaching duties also require that I develop activities to use during class, meet with students, create and grade exams and assignments, review potential textbooks, and update my course Web sites. I probably spend about 30 to 40 percent of my time in teaching-related activities. Research occupies most of my time. This involves reading books and research articles, designing research studies, collecting and analyzing data, writing reports for completed research projects, creating grant proposals, and doing other types of writing (such as this book). Research occupies about 50 percent of my time (or more when deadlines loom). The remainder of my time I spend on various professional activities, which include attending department meetings, serving on committees at UT or for professional organizations, reviewing manuscripts for research journals, and providing my expertise to individuals and organizations that might benefit from it.

Professional Paths

Because the professions related to motor behavior are so diverse, each career path has its own unique characteristics. Many professional paths have employment opportunities that require less education than the academic path. This section focuses on two professional paths—physical education and occupational therapy—to illustrate some of the possibilities available.

Physical Educator

To become a physical educator, you will typically need to complete an undergraduate degree in physical education. These programs often include components in health education as well. In addition to learning about the physical and psychological foundations of movement in classes such as exercise physiology and exercise psychology, you will learn about specific ways of teaching physical education classes. You will also need to gain proficiency in a wide variety of sports and movement-related games, so you will take several physical activity courses. *Pedagogy* classes will provide you with an understanding of different teaching methods, and a period of student teaching will ensure that you can put these ideas into practice.

TECHNOLOGY HIGHLIGHT

Motion Capture

Motion capture is the process of recording the position, in three dimensions, of specific locations on the body during the execution of movement skills. When these positions are recorded rapidly enough, scientists can gather accurate information regarding various aspects of human movement such as the speed of limb movements, changes in direction, and sequencing of actions. Still pictures and then film and video recordings were the early technologies used in this type of measurement (see the highlight on Muybridge at the end of chapter 1). Today, motion capture devices can incorporate a variety of technologies that detect information mechanically, optically, or electromagnetically. Optically based motion capture systems are probably the most widely used. They record information by detecting light waves from markers placed on the body. Some systems bounce light off highly reflective markers, while other systems use markers that actually give off light themselves. When sensors are placed on several sides of a performer, motion capture systems can track very complex movements that would be difficult to study otherwise.

Motion capture is also used by animators and filmmakers to re-create realistic movements of imaginary characters. Filmmakers created the movements of the character Gollum in the *Lord of the Rings* movie series by capturing the motions of a human actor and translating them to produce a creature that was distinctly not human yet moved in human ways.

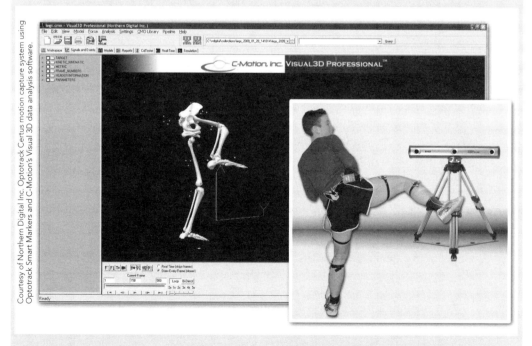

Courtesy of Northern Digital Inc. Optotrack Certus motion capture system using Optotrack Smart Markers and C-Motion's Visual 3D data analysis software.

An optical motion capture system from Northern Digital Inc. is used to record the movements of a participant (right panel) and send them to a software interface (left panel) for display and analysis.

Most physical education programs include courses on motor learning to ensure that their students understand the principles of movement control and skill learning. In addition, motor development is often required because most positions involve teaching children. In most cases, you will need to take a licensing exam to become a physical education teacher.

There are few things that you can't do as long as you are willing to apply yourself.

Greg LeMond

As a physical educator, your job will involve teaching physical education classes for most of the school day (PE Central, 2007). You may also be assigned to teach health classes or another subject if you have the appropriate qualifications. The number of classes you teach in a day will depend upon the school system you work in and whether you teach at the elementary or the secondary level. In the United States, the elementary level usually encompasses kindergarten through fifth grade. In many elementary schools, physical education is taught in short classes (e.g., 30 minutes) throughout the day. The secondary level usually encompasses sixth through 12th grades. In some regions, intermediate schools include sixth through eighth grade and high schools include ninth through 12th grade. Teaching at the secondary level typically involves several full class periods each day.

Physical educators often do not get much time during the day to complete planning and other activities needed to support their teaching. As a result, your day might start fairly early so that you can organize equipment and prepare facilities, and you may need to devote some of your evenings to creating lesson plans (especially early in your career). The good news is that your workday will probably end sometime in the afternoon. During class, your primary focus will be on teaching your students various movement skills, sports, games, and other physical activities. At the elementary level, you will often focus on activities and games that teach fundamental motor skills such as throwing, rolling, kicking, and catching balls, as well as running, jumping, hopping, and skipping. If you teach older students, you will focus more on teaching sports and other lifetime physical activities (e.g., strength training and dance). These types of activities will include instruction regarding rules of the game or guidelines for participation as well as the movement skills themselves.

You can find more information about physical education as a career by visiting these Web sites:

- Association for Physical Education (England): www.afpe.org.uk
- Education-Portal.com: http://education-portal.com/articles/Career_Information_for_a_Degree_in_Physical_Education.html
- myfuture (Australia): www.myfuture.edu.au/services/default.asp?FunctionID=5050&ASCO=241000A

- PE Central: www.pecentral.org
- University of North Carolina Wilmington Career Center: www.uncwil.edu/stuaff/career/Majors/physed.htm#whatis

Occupational Therapist

Occupational therapy is a rehabilitation profession that strives to help disabled people regain the skills needed for independent living (American Occupational Therapy Association, 2007; Bureau of Labor Statistics, U.S. Department of Labor, 2007). These skills vary depending upon the individual patient and circumstances of the impairment. For example, a child with an attention disorder will need different treatment than an adult attempting to recover the capability to speak after a stroke. Becoming an occupational therapist requires a bachelor's degree followed by a graduate degree in occupational therapy. It is important that you determine entrance requirements for the program you are considering so that you can take the prerequisite courses during your undergraduate program. Majors such as kinesiology, biology, and psychology are common starting points; but other majors can work provided that the requirements for the graduate program are met. There are two options for graduate education. The first is a master's degree program that prepares you for an entry-level position as an occupational therapist. The second is a doctoral program, which requires additional work and a research component. Both degrees require supervised fieldwork to ensure that you can put your knowledge and skills into practice in an effective manner. In addition to obtaining your education, you will take a national certification exam.

The expectations of life depend upon diligence; the mechanic that would perfect his work must first sharpen his tools.

Confucius

As an occupational therapist, you will spend your day evaluating and working with patients. The activities on which you might focus encompass virtually every aspect of daily living, so the range of tasks you work with will be quite broad. For example, you might help a patient with problems in using a cell phone, bathing and dressing, completing tasks at school, or driving a car. You might address issues related to movement (e.g., coordination and timing), vision (e.g., visual acuity), memory, decision making, and strength and conditioning. In addition to working with patients, you might also evaluate living and work environments so that they can be modified to facilitate your patient's progress toward independence. These modifications might be physical changes to the environment (adding hold bars), changes to the task demands (e.g., incorporating breaks), or changes to the types of activities your patient engages in.

Some occupational therapists specialize in one area of practice. For example, you might help people return to work after some disabling event such as an accident or illness, or you might help disabled people enter the workforce for the first time. In both cases, you will likely work with employers to modify the work environment, help your patients find employment, and track their progress. You might also specialize in a specific type of disability. For example, you may work exclusively with people who have attention disorders. This might seem unrelated to motor behavior, but in fact some children with attention disorders also have difficulties with motor skills. Finally, you might focus on a specific segment of the population. For example, you might work with older adults in addressing issues related to physical function (e.g., walking and rising from a chair), memory (e.g., effectively managing their medications), and transportation (e.g., driving or using public transportation).

You can find more information about occupational therapy as a career by visiting these Web sites:

- American Occupational Therapy Association: www.aota.org/featured/area2/links/link09.asp
- Australian Association of Occupational Therapists WA: www.otauswa.com.au/index.cfm?objectid=C0CBD54C-1422-130F-33874A97B78481A1
- Canadian Association of Occupational Therapists: www.caot.ca/default.asp?pageid=285
- U.S. Department of Labor *Occupational Outlook Handbook:* www.bls.gov/oco/ocos078.htm
- U.S. News & World Report *Best Careers 2009* article on occupational therapy: www.usnews.com/articles/business/best-careers/2008/12/11/best-careers-2009-occupational-therapist.html

Side Paths

Apart from the more traditional academic and professional career paths, there are other creative paths to a career in motor behavior that you are probably not as familiar with. Two of the newer types of professionals in this field are the human performance consultant and the skill acquisition specialist.

Human Performance Consultant

To work as a *human performance consultant,* you will need a great deal of flexibility in your capability to apply principles of motor behavior to solve practical problems for your clients. Because the range of topics you address will vary according to the clients for whom you work, you will likely need to be able to quickly learn the basics of your client's industry. Many consultants work as freelancers, acting as the owner of their own business, which means that their success depends largely on their understanding of business principles as well as the principles they use to study movement problems for their clients. Many human performance consultants hold doctorates in fields related to motor behavior, but there is no

consultant—A professional with specialized knowledge who provides his or her expertise to clients, usually on a project-by-project basis.

formal requirement that this be the case. Some larger companies that specialize in consulting may hire individuals with bachelor's or master's degrees and promote them on the basis of how well they perform for clients. Higher levels of education will typically give you an advantage because good graduate programs impart an understanding of how to systematically address movement-related problems and use a variety of measurement technologies.

As a **consultant,** your work will vary widely depending upon your clients' needs. For example, one day you might be hired by an auto manufacturer to demonstrate that the layout of an instrument panel does not interfere with a driver's capability to monitor the road. Another day, you might be hired to complete a forensic analysis of a portable crib that collapsed and killed a child. On yet another day, you might find yourself working on a project to refine a warning label for a hair dryer, or testing the interface of a computer software product. Your job will depend on effective communication with your clients and other interested parties. Some of this communication might involve initial meetings (possibly even including sales), producing written reports, giving verbal presentations, and testifying in court cases. In addition, you will be designing ways to test products such as the portable crib, or coming up with ideas about the causes of behavior—for example, examining how the design of a car can prevent sudden acceleration accidents.

You should note that there is no widely accepted label for what I have called a human performance consultant. Similar jobs might be associated with terms such as *human factors, ergonomics,* or *usability.* In fact, you will encounter these three terms fairly often if you are looking to work for a large consulting firm (e.g., Exponent) or in an industry that regularly employs people to examine human performance as it relates to their products and services.

You can learn more about consulting and jobs examining human performance in industry (e.g., human factors, ergonomics, and usability) by visiting the following Web sites.

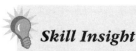

Skill Insight

Driving a compact tractor is a complex motor skill. Tractors made by a company called Bobcat are controlled by two hand levers and two foot pedals. The hand levers are used to control the direction of the tractor. Pushing both levers forward or backward will make the tractor move in the corresponding direction. To make the tractor turn right, you pull back on the right lever and push forward on the left. To make it turn left, you switch the arms that are pushing and pulling. One of the foot pedals raises and lowers the bucket arm while the other controls the scooping and dumping action of the bucket. Picking up a scoop of dirt requires the simultaneous control of both hand levers and both foot pedals, which can quickly overload a person's capability to pay attention to everything at the same time. For example, it is very easy to focus on the scooping action of the bucket and forget that you are still lowering the bucket arm and trying to drive forward. If this is not corrected, the tractor can actually tip itself backward to the point that it flips upside down. Some novice users find that they actually need to release both handles and lift their feet off the pedals when they feel that they are losing control of the tractor.

- Exponent: www.exponent.com/ (Look for the section on Human Factors.)
- Human Performance Research: www.hp-research.com/
- U.S. News & World Report *Best Careers 2009* article on usability: www.usnews.com/articles/business/best-careers/2008/12/11/best-careers-2009-usability-experience-specialist.html
- The Usability Professionals' Organization: www.upassoc.org/
- Human Factors & Ergonomics Society: www.hfes.org
- The Ergonomics Society (England): www.ergonomics.org.uk/
- Gesellschaft für Arbeitswissenschaft (Germany): www.gfa-online.de/index.php
- The Inter-Regional Ergonomic Association (Russia): www.ergo-org.ru/

Skill Acquisition Specialist

The Australian Institute of Sport (AIS) employs two skill acquisition specialists, a career that may become more common worldwide in the future. The AIS was founded in the 1980s to help develop high-performance athletes who represent Australia at international competitions such as the Olympics. As a skill acquisition specialist, you would work with athletes from a wide variety of sports and apply your understanding of motor behavior to an equally wide variety of performance and learning issues. One of the skill acquisition specialists currently employed by the AIS has a bachelor's degree and a graduate diploma in human movement with a specialization in skill acquisition (note that a graduate diploma is awarded for graduate work but does not reflect as much training as a master's degree). The other one has a bachelor's degree in coaching science and a master's degree in sport psychology and is pursuing a doctorate in skill acquisition.

In this type of position, you will likely work on several projects throughout the year and perhaps even more than one at a time. For example, on one project you might work with the women's volleyball team to enhance their decision-making skills when blocking opponents' shots. On another, you might evaluate the relative merits of video simulations that use either an athlete point of view or a bird's-eye view to depict an unfolding play. On yet another project, you might help a gymnastics coach to implement a practice drill that incorporates the benefits of self-controlled feedback. According to the AIS, their skill acquisition team focuses on practical methods to enhance performance. These include developing innovative practice techniques, evaluating various technological approaches to skill learning (e.g., video simulation), consulting with coaches, and identifying ways to help athletes effectively use sensory information during the performance of their sport.

You can find more information about the AIS by visiting their Web site (www.ausport.gov.au/ais).

I believe that opportunities for *side path* careers such as human performance consultant and skill acquisition specialist will expand in the future, particularly as they relate to the use of video analysis. Several companies produce software programs that will allow you to capture video to a computer and then analyze the motion in several ways. Programs such as Dartfish and Silicon Coach are fairly inexpensive

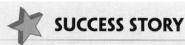

SUCCESS STORY

Richard Schmidt, Human Performance Research

Richard A. Schmidt, PhD, runs a company called Human Performance Research. Through this company, Dr. Schmidt provides consulting in human performance, human factors and ergonomics, and human learning and training. In his career, Dr. Schmidt has consulted on issues of human performance related to automobile accidents, vehicle design (e.g., how far apart to space the accelerator and brake pedals), product labeling, accidental discharge of firearms, lighting and visibility, and the design of sport and exercise equipment. In addition, he has consulted on issues related to training and learning of skills in industrial settings.

Photo courtesy of Richard Schmidt.

Consulting on this scale is often the result of many years of experience as an established researcher. Indeed, Dr. Schmidt came to consulting through his career as an academic researcher—he is one of the most widely published and influential researchers in motor behavior and has authored two of the most frequently used textbooks on motor learning and control. He began his academic path at the University of California at Berkeley, where he earned bachelor's and master's degrees in physical education. He then earned his doctoral degree in physical education from the University of Illinois. During his career as an academic, Dr. Schmidt worked at the University of Maryland, University of Michigan, University of Southern California, and University of California at Los Angeles. Early in his career, he primarily focused on issues related to physical education, but his interests eventually drifted toward psychology and then psychological aspects of human factors. He finished his academic career as a professor of psychology at UCLA in 1998. He has been an extremely productive researcher throughout his career, publishing over 150 research articles and writing several books. Although Dr. Schmidt began consulting while he was still an academic, he had accumulated about 15 years of professional experience before taking on his first consulting project.

and easy to use. The wide availability of video cameras will allow video analysts to provide services to a range of smaller-scale clients such as public schools, sport club coaches, or small business owners. I have used video analysis in two of my recent studies, one on the *takeoff* maneuver in surfing (Fairbrother & Boxell, 2008) and the other on the capability of young children to collapse a portable crib while inside of it (Fairbrother, Readdick, & Shea, 2008).

The Short of It

- The term motor behavior refers both to an academic field and to the general phenomenon that human behavior often involves movement. Accordingly, knowledge of the principles of motor behavior is useful in any professional career that deals with human movement.

- The academic career path resulting in a college or university position as an assistant professor requires extensive education. Typically, entry-level professor positions require the equivalent of bachelor's, master's, and doctoral degrees, which take about eight or more years to obtain. In addition, some researchers serve for one or more years in a postdoctoral position prior to their first job as an assistant professor.

- There are many professional career paths that are closely aligned with the study of motor behavior. Among these are physical educator, coach, occupational therapist, physical therapist, and human factors specialist.

- Providing consulting services using knowledge of motor behavior is a side path either to a career as a human performance consultant or a skill acquisition specialist, or to a part-time job that will generate additional income. Widely available and easy-to-use video analysis systems provide one way to examine human movements and help clients improve their performance.

II
PART

Building Blocks of Motor Behavior

In part II, you will learn about the basic concepts and principles related to motor behavior. These are called the building blocks because they will help you establish a strong foundation of knowledge should you decide to pursue a career concerned with movement. Chapter 3 discusses the process of observation on which the study of motor behavior is based. Chapter 4 introduces you to how people control their movements, and chapter 5 describes some of the ways in which people learn motor skills. Chapter 6 discusses a range of human capabilities and limitations in meeting certain task demands. Chapter 7 describes the various ways in which practice settings can be structured. Chapter 8 introduces the motor skill learning cycle, which can be used as a guide to developing effective instruction for movement skills. Finally, the epilogue suggests future directions for the field of motor behavior. Before we begin with these topics, however, I want to outline a few basic themes that tie all of the concepts together. If the chapters are the building blocks, you can think of these themes as the mortar used to bind the blocks together into a sturdy body of knowledge.

Taking a Systematic Approach

The first theme is that it is best to use a systematic approach to examine the factors that influence how people perform and learn motor skills. There are four basic steps in adopting such an approach:

1. Identify the behavior you want to better understand.
2. Identify the factors that influence this behavior.
3. Either control or measure important factors to see how the behavior changes when the factors change.
4. Make multiple observations of the behavior as you study it.

The first step in our systematic approach is to identify the actual behavior we want to better understand. Is it baseball pitching performance during an important game? Is it how the quality of an exerciser's form changes when he or she is working out in a novel environment (e.g., in a gym with mirrors compared to at home)? Is it the amount of time a swimmer takes in completing a flip turn? After we choose the behavior to study, the second step is to identify factors that might influence it. One way to do this is to think about who will be performing the task and what the task demands of this person. Then, we can think about how the performance setting might influence the performer or change the task demands. In this discussion, we are simply using the term *factor* as a short way of referring to either a characteristic (of the person or the task) or a circumstance (in which performance occurs). You'll learn more about these three factors—the person, the task, and the setting—in the next section.

If we think a factor will influence the behavior we are studying, our third step is to either control it or measure it. Often, we can just determine if a given factor is present or not. For example, when we shoot free throws, we can either have an audience or not. So, if we want to study the effects of an audience on free throw shooting, we can compare performances with and without an audience. In this case, we have controlled the factor (the audience) to see how it influences the behavior we are examining (free throw shooting). At other times, we will have no way to control a factor and so all we can do is measure it. For example, performance in downhill ski racing can be greatly affected by outside temperature. Even a few degrees can change the consistency of the snow, which in turn will influence how a skier completes his or her turns. Because there is no way to control the temperature on a ski slope, we would simply measure it and see how changes in temperature related to changes in performance.

The fourth step in our systematic approach is to make multiple observations. If we observe something only a few times, we might not get an accurate picture of the behavior we want to understand. The more times we observe a behavior, the more likely it is that we understand it. For example, suppose we notice that our favorite baseball pitcher suddenly loses accuracy after about four innings. We might be tempted to chalk this up to physical fatigue, but we need to be careful. Unless we watch him enough times to see that his wild pitching really is related to the number of pitches he has thrown, we can't rule out other causes (such as changes in the batting lineup that force him to throw his weaker pitches).

Accounting for the Person, the Task, and the Performance Setting

The second theme running throughout this book relates to the importance of accounting for the various influences arising from the characteristics of the performer, the demands of the task and the performance setting, and the ways in which these three factors interact. Remember, this is the second step in our systematic approach. One way to view the relationships among these factors is to think of the entire performance situation as a puzzle assembled from a number of pieces. The figure below is a graphic representation of this idea. In the center, you see the PERSON represented by the light gray puzzle pieces and the TASK represented by the white pieces. These are interlocked to represent the interaction of the person with the task. When we are trying to understand motor behavior, it does not make sense to consider the person without the task because the task is what requires movement.

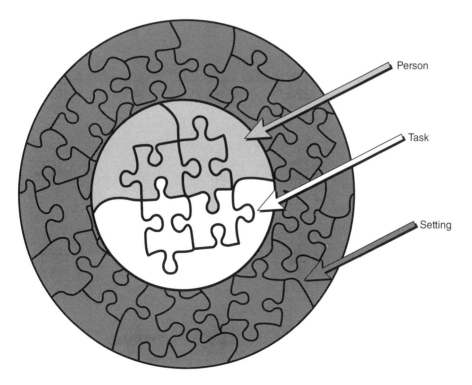

The person, task, and setting all interact to influence a person's performance.

Similarly, examining the task alone does not make sense because a person is needed to perform it. The inner circle consisting of the person engaged with the task is embedded in a larger circle of dark gray puzzle pieces that represent the PERFORMANCE SETTING in which the person performs the task. Each of the three sections of the overall puzzle has multiple pieces to indicate that the person, the task, and the setting all have many dimensions worth considering. For example, the puzzle pieces for a person might include age, experience, and personality traits. For the task, the puzzle pieces might include decision making, coordination of multiple limbs, and precise timing. For the setting, the pieces might include the weather (assuming the task is to be performed outdoors), the presence of an audience, and consequences of the performance (e.g., is it a competition or practice?).

From this perspective, motor behavior can be seen as a product of these elements:

1. The capabilities and limitations of the person
2. The demands of the task
3. The influence of the setting

Here is an example from the sport of soccer, in which a goalkeeper is working to improve her skills in defending penalty kicks. Using the systematic approach described earlier, her coach will want to consider the factors that will be most likely to influence the goalkeeper's performance. First, the coach should consider her capabilities and limitations as they relate to the skill of blocking penalty kicks. Two important ingredients for success in this task are the goalkeeper's capability to predict the direction of the kick and the speed of her response (e.g., a dive). Her coach will want to assess both of these aspects to determine which one needs the most work. For example, maybe the goalkeeper is fast enough but has a hard time predicting direction. The speed of her dive won't help much if she goes in the wrong direction or simply starts too late.

Next, the coach should consider the task demands of blocking a kick. The difficulty of this task will depend on the skill level of the player taking the kick. Some players are very good at hiding their kick direction. If they also have a very powerful kick, the goalkeeper has very little time to make a decision and then respond. Finally, the coach should consider the performance setting because the goalkeeper's performance will often depend upon the situation. Defending a penalty kick during a game is different than during practice. During the game, there are negative consequences to not blocking a shot, but missing shots during practice is a normal part of the learning process. If the coach really challenges the player, we might expect the goalkeeper to miss many of the shots during practice but block most of them during the game.

The coach can use our systematic approach to determine which aspects of the goalkeeper's performance need the most work. A way to do this is to hold some factors constant during practice drills while varying others. To test the goalkeeper's response speed, for example, the coach can have her defend predictable shots taken by different players. If the goalkeeper's performance drops noticeably when she faces the strongest kickers, then she needs to work on her speed. To test the goalkeeper's skill at predicting the direction of the shots, the coach can have her face players who are good at disguising their shots. If the goalkeeper hesitates or moves in the wrong direction, then she needs to work on her prediction skills.

Information Processing

The third and final theme I will introduce in this section relates to how humans use information from the environment to guide their actions. This perspective is commonly called an information processing approach. I will explain this in more detail in chapter 6, but you will find a basic understanding of it useful as you read chapters 3 through 5. The idea is that we extract information from our perceptions of the environment, use that information to make decisions about the appropriate response, and then prepare our bodies to execute the response. The simplest model of information processing involves three stages:

1. Stimulus identification
2. Response selection
3. Response programming

All three of these processes occur during a period of time known as reaction time. Reaction time is the amount of time that passes from the moment an unexpected cue is detected until movement begins. Your reaction time, then, is how long it takes you to *begin* a movement response, not how long it actually takes you to respond. Step 2 of our systematic approach (accounting for the person, task, and setting) illustrates how information processing works. Everyone has certain capabilities and limitations in terms of how he or she processes information. For example, even though all the members of a basketball team can see the same things on the court, some players will be quicker than others to notice when the other team is running a given play. Our capabilities and limitations interact with the information processing demands created by the task and the performance setting. For example, a player who has a better view of the court because of his position will have an advantage in detecting a play.

Let's return to our soccer example to see how each of the three stages of information processing works. During the first stage (stimulus identification), the goalkeeper detects information from her environment. This will most likely consist of cues related to the movements of the kicker and the ball. Once she gathers that information, the goalkeeper will complete the second stage (response selection). During response selection, she will decide when and how to respond (to block the kick). Finally, she will complete the third stage (response programming). During this stage, the goalkeeper's brain and central nervous system will create a set of instructions to tell her body how to move. These instructions will then be sent to her muscles, which will act to produce the movements she planned.

Remember, all three stages happen before the goalkeeper even begins to move. So, the longer it takes her to complete her information processing, the less time she will have to actually move before the ball passes the goal line. In later chapters, you will learn about some of the factors that influence each stage of information processing to either speed up or slow down reaction time. You will also learn about training strategies that allow people to reduce the amount of time they spend processing information. One of the most helpful of these is anticipation because it allows you to decide what you are going to do (i.e., complete the response selection stage) before you even receive the cue to act. You will also learn about how task demands and performance settings can influence information processing. For example, ice hockey emphasizes rapid decision making, while darts emphasizes methodical aiming. Although not all of our movement responses require information processing as outlined in this model, I think you will find the model a very useful approach to understanding motor behavior.

CHAPTER 3

Observing Behavior

✓ The aspects of information processing that are emphasized when a motor skill is performed in a predictable setting

✓ The aspects of information processing that are emphasized when a motor skill is performed in a changing and unpredictable setting

✓ How different task demands related to the time it takes to execute a skill influence the way we control our movements

✓ How researchers and professionals use observation to understand motor behavior

> A few observations and much reasoning lead to error; many observations and a little reasoning to truth.
>
> **Alexis Carrel**

When I was in college, I worked as a bartender to help pay my bills. To become a bartender, I needed to master a few fundamental skills. The most important of these was the "free pour," which requires a bartender to pour a shot of liquor from a bottle into a glass. Each bottle in the bar was fitted with a pour spout that allowed the fluid to flow freely in a small stream when the bottle was inverted. There are several tricks to a free pour. First, the bartender must know how to invert the bottle rapidly so that drinks can be made as quickly as possible without spilling. Second, the bartender must know how long to hold the pour to get exactly one shot into the glass. This particular aspect of the skill is quite challenging because the rate of flow is affected by both the thickness of the liquor and the amount in the bottle. Third, the bartender must quickly end the flow of fluid with a rapid rotation of the wrist while simultaneously turning the bottle back to upright.

The way my boss trained me illustrates that he was quite good at observing behavior and setting up appropriate challenges to help me master the skills needed to bartend. He first filled a bottle with water and had me practice pouring shots into several different types of glasses. The different glasses prevented me from using a visual cue on a specific type of glass to gauge my pour. He wanted me to learn how to "feel" the pour without relying on vision, because once I got on the job I would not be able to rely on vision. A shot poured into two identical glasses can look very different because the ice is never exactly the same in both glasses. In addition, a bartender needs to be able to look at customers while pouring drinks. My boss watched me practice and gave me feedback about what I was doing correctly and incorrectly. Once I learned how to free pour, he allowed me to bartend when business was slow and challenged me by talking while I filled drink orders. Because an effective and fast bartender needs to use both hands simultaneously, he would always ask what I was doing with my other hand when he saw me only using one hand to pour drinks.

This chapter describes how we observe behavior to better understand the ways in which people control movements and learn motor skills. My boss watched me and provided feedback to help me learn the skill of free pouring. Similarly, researchers observe movements to discover the factors that affect how we control our movements or learn motor skills. Other professionals such as coaches or therapists use observation for the same reason as my boss—to monitor the progress of their athletes or patients in performing important motor skills and use this information to provide the right types of instructional support.

It is important to remember that all movement skills have what might be called a set of general demands. In everyday language, we might say that a skill involves moving an object (such as a rugby ball), running, coordinating our limbs (as in a tennis serve), or some other general demand (or combination of demands). These demands are what actually define the required actions for the skill. For example, taking a penalty kick requires running for the approach, the coordination of limbs to correctly time the movements of the support and kicking legs, even more coordination of the limbs to use the upper body to offset the kicking motion (so you follow through instead of falling down), and the capability to make the ball travel both fast and accurately.

One good approach to identifying these demands is through a process called *skill classification*. The point of skill classification is to discover the nature of task demands so that we might consider the ways in which these demands will influence performance and how we prepare for performance. In other words, the goal is not just to recognize that bowling is a *closed skill,* but to recognize that because bowling is a closed skill it emphasizes the careful execution of movements rather than rapid decision making under a time pressure as in many *open skills*. Although there are several different classification schemes, the chapter focuses on two schemes that I think emphasize important considerations one needs to keep in mind when trying to understand task demands related to motor behavior.

Closed and Open Skills

The first classification scheme is one based upon the relative predictability of events that occur within the performance setting. In this scheme, skills that are performed in relatively predictable settings are called **closed skills** while skills performed in relatively unpredictable settings are called **open skills** (Poulton, 1954). Good examples of closed skills can be seen in most of the exercises that a physical therapist might prescribe to strengthen the rotator cuff muscles of an injured shoulder. The typical physical therapy setting is extremely predictable because the emphasis is on movement quality. A good example of an open skill is snowboarding on a crowded ski slope. Several aspects of the performance setting change in somewhat unpredictable ways. Probably the most important of these is the behavior of the other skiers and snowboarders. As you travel down the slope, you must constantly watch for other people crossing your path so that you can avoid a collision. It is important to recognize that the terms closed and open represent two ends of a range of predictability in the setting rather than two distinct categories (see figure 3.1).

closed skills—Skills that take place in performance settings that are predictable.

open skills—Skills that take place in performance settings that are unpredictable.

FIGURE 3.1 A depiction of the classification of skills based upon the range of predictability in the performance setting.

So, we can think of a skill as relatively closed or relatively open in comparison to other skills that might fall closer to the other end of the range.

When using the open–closed classification scheme, remember that the amount of time available to react to changes in the performance setting affects how you should think about the demands of the skill. For example, if a marksman is presented with a random series of targets, we might think of the skill involved as an open skill. On the other hand, if he has unlimited time to prepare for each shot, the demands of the task more closely resemble those for a closed skill. The take-home message for this type of skill classification is that it allows you to understand how different types of skills emphasize different aspects of performance. Open skills tend to emphasize rapid decision making once a cue to begin the skill has been presented. Thus, the first two stages of information processing that I described in the introduction to part II of this book—stimulus identification and response selection—play important roles in determining the success of the action. For example, during a passing play in American football, the quarterback must read the defense, monitor his own receivers, and decide where to throw the ball. This performance setting involves a high degree of unpredictability because the quarterback has no way of knowing in advance how well any particular receiver will be covered by the defense. In addition, there is a tremendous pressure to throw the ball quickly to avoid the pass rush of the defending team.

 I don't dawdle. I'm a surgeon. I make an incision, do what needs to be done, and sew up the wound. There is a beginning, middle, and end.

Richard Selzer

Closed skills tend to emphasize careful preparation and execution of the movement response. The third stage of information processing—response programming—is usually the most important in closed skills. Imagine that you are driving a forklift to place pallets of a product into the back of a tractor trailer (see figure 3.2). Your job is to move the pallets from one location to another, then lift them to the appropriate level and carefully position them inside the back of the truck. To prevent the pallets from falling, you must take great care in moving the controls in order to position the forks so that the weight of the pallet is distributed evenly. Once you get the pallet, you need to carefully turn the forklift and drive to the truck. At the truck, you

© picsfive/Fotolia.com

FIGURE 3.2 Lifting a pallet with a forklift is considered a closed skill because it does not require much in the way of stimulus identification or response selection.

need to precisely align the forklift with the door opening, elevate the pallet to the correct height, slowly move forward, and then gently lower the pallet and reverse the forklift. The primary demand of this job is related to the precision with which your movements (of the steering wheel, foot pedals, and other control knobs) result in an efficient and controlled operation of the forklift. Stimulus identification and response selection do not impose many demands in this example. You can focus on one pallet at a time, and there is no unpredictability about your interaction with the pallet. The emphasis instead is on carefully preparing and executing each of your movements to control the forklift.

Understanding the range of predictability represented by the open and closed skill classification scheme is extremely useful to professionals when they think about the best ways to deliver motor skill instruction. It may seem fairly straightforward that training for relatively open skills should emphasize decision making. While this is generally true, it is probably a bit too simplistic. Even skills that are very open require the preparation and execution of the appropriate movement response. In training for open skills, it is very common to reduce or remove the decision-making demands for early learners. A good example of this is when we teach a child to hit a baseball from a tee. This strategy allows the child to focus on acquiring the correct movement. Once a certain level of proficiency has been reached, other demands can gradually be introduced. When they simplify open skills for early learners, instructors should remember that these learners will eventually need to perform in real-world settings that require decision making.

For relatively closed skills, an instructor would not want to introduce stimulus identification or response selection demands because they typically would not be part of the setting in which the skill will ultimately be performed. Extremely complex skills, however, might be simplified in some way to initially reduce the response programming demand. For example, a dance instructor might teach just the first few steps of a dance to a beginner. As the learner progresses, additional elements can then be incorporated. As with any skill, the instructor will eventually want to incorporate the full range of demands that will exist in the typical performance setting.

 Those move easiest who have learn'd to dance.

Alexander Pope

Because the open and closed skill classification scheme represents a range rather than two distinct categories, it is important to recognize that predictability will differ from task to task, and will often change for a given task depending on the time or place in which it is performed (i.e., the performance setting). Consider a server in a restaurant carrying a tray with a glass of water and a cup of coffee on it. If she is delivering these drinks to the first table of the night and the restaurant is fairly empty, she will not face many surprises (that is, the skill is a relatively closed skill). As the restaurant gets busier, she will have to contend with the movements of customers and other restaurant employees. This will add an element of uncertainty and make the skill a bit more open, but most of the time this will not be much of a challenge if she remains alert. In this case, the skill would probably fall about midway between the two ends of the range from closed to open skills.

Now imagine that the server is working on a night when several local high schools are holding their annual dance. The restaurant is exceptionally crowded with teenagers who are continually jumping up to visit their friends at other tables. In some spots, the people might actually be standing elbow to elbow. The movements of all these people in close proximity will increase the unpredictability of the performance setting, making carrying a tray a very open skill. The server is also likely to encounter—in addition to people bumping into her or her tray—a "helpful" customer who will unexpectedly lift one of the glasses and upset the balance of the tray. If this happens, she will have to respond rapidly to compensate for the suddenly uneven distribution of weight on the tray.

Some skills, such as driving a car, have components that are more open and also some that are more closed. For example, parking your car in an uncrowded lot is a relatively closed skill, whereas parallel parking on a busy street is more of an open skill. The key to categorizing the skill is to carefully consider a variety of realistic situations in which the skill might be performed and then identify the ones that are most likely to present the performer with critical challenges. Also remember that our focus here is on the unpredictability of the performance setting only. It is understandable to see the performance of a novice as unpredictable (you should see me juggle), but this does not make the task an open skill. For example, if I ask you to throw darts using your nondominant hand, it is unlikely that you will be able to precisely predict where the dart will land. However, this would still be a closed skill because the performance setting does not introduce any uncertainty that you need to respond to during the act of throwing the darts.

Skill Insight

Learning a motor skill can change your brain. Bogdan Draganski and colleagues (Draganski et al., 2004) used three-dimensional magnetic resonance imaging to examine the brains of 12 people who were given three months to learn to juggle three balls. The jugglers' brains were scanned before practice began, then after they could juggle for 60 seconds, and then a final time three months after the practice period ended. Similar scans were made for a group of nonjugglers. At the beginning of the experiment, there were no differences in brain anatomy between the two groups. Once the jugglers had practiced enough to keep the balls in the air for 60 seconds, however, their brains showed anatomical changes in specific areas used in the skill of juggling. At the final scan (three months after their learning experience) most of the jugglers had not maintained their skill and their brains no longer differed from those of the nonjugglers. This study illustrates two important points. First, it shows that the brain actually grows in response to task demands (much like other parts of the body). Second, it reminds us that positive changes can disappear when we stop practicing our skills.

Discrete, Serial, and Continuous Skills

The second classification scheme relates to the ways in which we use information in preparing and correcting our movements (Schmidt & Lee, 2005). As with the open and closed skill classification scheme, the discrete and continuous classifications are typically thought to represent two ends of a range, with the serial classification falling in the middle. **Discrete skills** are those that have a readily identifiable beginning and end. Examples include swinging a baseball bat, flipping an egg, and plucking a string on a guitar. **Continuous skills** are those without readily identifiable beginning and ending points. Examples include tracing a drawing, cutting a pattern with a power jigsaw, and swimming. **Serial skills** are those that string together a series of discrete actions. Examples include typing, playing a video game that requires you to use a joystick and buttons, and playing a chord change on a guitar.

discrete skill—A skill that has a distinct beginning and ending; these skills are often performed rapidly.

serial skill—A skill that consists of a sequence of discrete actions; sometimes one of the components in the sequence might be continuous, for example the approach run in the pole vault.

continuous skill—A skill that does not have distinct beginning and ending points.

I had the commitment, and I had the understanding, that the basis of football is skill on the ball, and if you spend the time with it, you're gonna reap the rewards.

Craig Johnston

Skill Insight

Variety may actually be the spice of life (well, for learning motor skills, anyway). When you learn more than one variation of a skill during a practice session, you will be more prepared to transfer the skill to a new variation than if you had simply practiced one variation. For example, practicing your tennis forehand by hitting to several locations on the court within a single session is a better idea than hitting down-the-line forehands one day, cross-court forehands on another day, and forehands to the middle on yet another day. Some research has suggested that this so-called *varied practice* could actually result in better learning than practice on a specific task, even when the varied practice did not include the specific task that was tested (Kerr & Booth, 1978).

The important thing about this classification scheme is not so much the qualities of the skill as indicated by the definitions, but the way the process of classification sheds light on how we use information in completing the skill (see figure 3.3). For example, discrete skills are generally completed quite rapidly, which means that the sensory information we receive from the environment or as a consequence of our movements can be used only in advance. Imagine hitting a nail with a hammer just one time. Once you have started the action, it is very difficult to adjust or stop. We can't process information fast enough to use it during rapid discrete actions such as this. On the other end of the spectrum are those tasks that unfold slowly enough for us to use information during the action. For slow continuous skills, we use information in two ways. First, we use it to adjust our impending actions by planning future movements that are part of the skill. For example, if you are running along a path in a park after a thunderstorm has knocked down tree branches, you will use visual information about these obstacles in your path to avoid them. The second way we use information is as feedback to correct ongoing movements. A good example of this can be seen in one of the aspects of driving a car. One of the goals of driving is to keep the car in the center of the lane you are driving in. As we invariably drift in one direction or another, our proximity to the lane line provides us feedback about our performance, which we can use to make a correction.

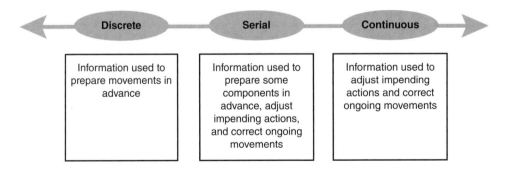

FIGURE 3.3 A depiction of the classification of skills based upon the way information is used to prepare, guide, and correct movements.

For serial skills, we often use information in all of the ways just described for discrete and continuous skills. This is because serial skills have features in common with both of the other types of skills. Many movements are a sequence of discrete actions, and for each of these actions, information can be used only for preplanning. However, because this string of actions often unfolds over a longer period of time, we can also use information in advance or as feedback for those aspects of the performance that relate to the unfolding sequence rather than to each individual discrete element. For example, when you hammer a nail, you typically hit it several times (instead of just once as in the example I used earlier). This sequence of discrete actions means that the real-world skill of hammering a nail could be considered a serial skill. Although you cannot adjust your movements during a single swing, you can adjust your aim or the amount of force you use to hit the nail on future swings. The implications of this classification scheme lead us to very important considerations regarding how we control our movements, which will be discussed in chapter 4, and how we use feedback to learn, which will be discussed in chapter 5.

Observation: A Critical Key to Understanding Motor Behavior

Now that you have some idea about how to use skill classification schemes to understand task demands, we can begin to talk about the process of observation. In addition to the identification of task demands, the observation process also involves the identification of the important elements of the movements we want to observe, such as the overall pattern of the movement, the timing characteristics, the sequencing of movements, and the limbs used to execute the movements.

Observation is simply the documentation of the behaviors displayed by performers as they engage in movement activities. When these behaviors are measurable, they can be used as an index of *motor performance.* Depending on the situation, measures of motor performance can be used to assess various aspects of motor behavior. For example, a physical therapist might measure a person's postural stability using a device that rapidly detects changes in how much force each foot applies to the ground. Then the therapist might use this measurement to determine if the patient's postural stability is normal for someone of the given age and activity level. Or a basketball coach might videotape athletes shooting free throws, record the number of baskets made, and measure their shooting form using a rating scale that helps to identify important aspects of free throw technique. While many coaches might simply watch their athletes, the use of video

observation—The act of documenting the behaviors displayed by a performer as he or she engages in a movement activity.

> *I finally decided on occupational therapy because I knew that this field would allow me to really help those who feel like they have lost everything.*
>
> **Kelly Andrasik**

is a fairly simple way to create a recording of observations that can then be viewed as many times as needed or even replayed in slow motion.

Observation is a necessary tool for understanding motor behavior. It can involve very sophisticated instrumentation as is often used in research settings, or it may consist of simply watching a performer and subjectively evaluating the movements

SUCCESS STORY

Daniel Walden, Professional Wakeboarder

Daniel Walden is a college student studying to become a physical therapist and is also a professional wakeboarder. At the time of this writing, Daniel is a student in my undergraduate motor behavior class, called Principles of Movement Control and Skill Learning. Although in the past he was not aware of the terminology and research from the field of motor behavior, Daniel's training philosophy embodies the application of many of the principles you will read about throughout this book. For example, Daniel identifies his extensive experience on the trampoline as one factor that helps him recognize what a new trick should "feel" like when he is in the air (Frances, 2006). This is a good example of how skilled performers use sensory information (in this case, the "feel") to help control their movements (you'll learn about this topic in chapter 4). This example also illustrates the principle of transfer of training: Because being in the air above a trampoline is similar to being in the air during a wakeboard trick, practice on one benefits performance on the other (you'll learn about this in chapter 5). Daniel also takes advantage of observational learning by watching his training partners and videos of other wakeboarders (chapter 5), as well as of simulation training using a device that pulls him on a cable instead of behind a boat (chapter 5). Finally, Daniel recognizes how arousal can negatively influence performance (chapter 6). He advises newer riders to not get frustrated (i.e., overly aroused) when training because this "clouds up" the mind.

Photo courtesy of Daniel Walden.

as is common in physical education and occupational therapy settings. For example, an occupational therapist might watch a patient who has lost his dominant arm as he learns to write with his remaining arm. If the patient has advanced to a certain skill level, the therapist might simply watch how he holds the pencil and provide feedback when she sees him drifting away from correct form.

To be helpful, we must know what to observe and how to interpret our observations. Before making any observations, it is good practice to precisely identify the behavior that we want to better understand. For example, if we want to understand how a surfer moves to a standing position after catching a wave (i.e., the *takeoff*), we should focus our observations on that portion of the activity. In addition, we would probably want to videotape the takeoff (see figure 3.4) so that we could slow down or stop the movement and examine it as many times as needed.

Preparation-to-stand (PTS)

Transition-to-standing (TTS)

Rail-release (RR)

FIGURE 3.4   Four frames from a video analysis of the surfing takeoff maneuver, showing the beginning and ending of three phases of the skill.

Journal of Behavior Analysis in Health, Sports, Fitness, and Medicine, © 2008 Behavior Analyst Online, Publisher, Journal of Behavior Analysis in Health, Sports, Fitness, and Medicine. From J.T. Fairbrother and R. Boxell, "The use of naturalistic observation to assess movement patterns and timing structure of the take-off maneuver in surfing," 1(1): 12-18.

Video-based observation is also used by human factors professionals. As one example, a company may need an evaluation of the postures that employees adopt when completing tasks that require lifting. Because some potentially harmful postures (e.g., not using the legs to lift) might be seen rather infrequently, it makes sense

TECHNOLOGY HIGHLIGHT

Video Observation and Movement Analysis

With just the use of a standard video camcorder, a personal computer, and a video analysis software package, you can unlock a tremendous amount of information about movements. Two popular software packages are Silicon Coach and Dartfish. These products allow you to digitally capture a video clip to a computer and then analyze it with a range of tools. For example, the image below shows a tennis player executing a serve. In this image, you can see that the player coordinates the ball toss with the movements of his racket arm. When one watches this event in person, it is often difficult to determine the exact timing of the toss with respect to the swing. The power of video analysis software is that it lets you examine still shots of movements over small increments of time. The surfing sequence in figure 3.4 on page 49 was captured using Silicon Coach. As you walk through each "frame" of the motion, the software allows you to estimate how much time it took to complete movements. In the surfing study (Fairbrother & Boxell, 2008), we discovered that it took our participants from .63 to 1.99 seconds to complete the takeoff, but the time to complete the transition to standing took only .15 to .60 seconds. So, we found out that the time it took to complete the transition to standing was very similar for all of the surfers, even on different waves and types of boards. If you implement the appropriate controls, video analysis software even allows you to calculate distances, velocities, and accelerations to gain an in-depth understanding of the movements you are studying.

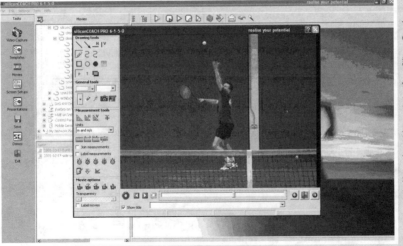

Image provided by author with permission from Silicon Coach.

The Silicon Coach interface as it was used to examine the tennis serve.

to videotape long periods of work and then rapidly review the footage to search for instances of the incorrect posture. The video also provides a record of an incident that might help the human factors professional understand the circumstances surrounding the use of an incorrect posture during lifting.

Observation can entail a variety of approaches to studying movements, ranging from laboratory examinations of participants learning novel tasks (e.g., pressing a sequence of keys on a computer keyboard in a prescribed amount of time), to field-based research (e.g., observation of surfing performance), and even to the use of existing data (e.g., using published U.S. Masters Swimming records to examine how swimming speed slows as athletes age) (Fairbrother, 2007a, b). It is during observation that we begin to apply the systematic approach and to account for the person, the task, and the performance setting as mentioned in the introduction to part II of this book. For example, we might use data sheets to record information about the performer such as age, experience, injury status, or skill level. We might also want to record information about the performance setting such as the facility, the opponent in a competition, or the weather if the performance occurs outside.

The Short of It

- Open skills emphasize decision making, while closed skills emphasize consistent preparation and execution of movements.

- We use information to guide our performance in different ways for different types of skills. For discrete skills, we use information to plan our actions in advance of the movement and as feedback for our next attempt. For continuous skills, we use information to plan for upcoming portions of our movement and also as feedback to help control our actions during the movement. For serial skills, we use information to plan our movements in advance and to modify upcoming portions of an unfolding movement sequence.

- Researchers and professionals use observation to understand motor behavior. Observation can take many forms, but is always designed to provide information about a selected aspect of a movement skill.

Understanding
How We
Control Movements

In this chapter you will learn the following:

✓ How we use information from different sources such as vision, balance, and touch to help control our movements
✓ How we control slow continuous movements using feedback
✓ How we control rapid discrete movements by planning them in advance

I consider skateboarding an art form, a lifestyle, and a sport.

Tony Hawk

A couple of years ago, I took on the project of assembling a play set for my daughter. This was one of those combination swing set, slide, sandbox, and clubhouse packages that you can buy at big wholesale clubs. During the assembly process, I got quite a bit of experience with various carpentry skills such as those involved in hammering nails, drilling holes, cutting boards, and driving screws. These types of tasks are fairly interesting from a motor behavior perspective: On the one hand they are simple enough to be accomplished by virtually anyone, but on the other hand, doing them in a manner that is both effective and efficient requires quite a bit of experience. For example, hammering a nail seems pretty simple (hold the nail with one hand and swing the hammer with the other), but have you ever considered how exactly this task is accomplished? The hand that holds the nail typically moves it into place, making several corrections to ensure that the tip is located in the right spot and that the nail is aligned straight up and down. Once the nail is in position, the other hand will quickly raise the hammer and forcefully lower it to apply the blow that drives the nail into the wood. Notice how the nail hand moves slowly while making many corrections whereas the hammer hand moves rapidly without making any changes along the way. Because the movement demands of the two hands differ so greatly, it makes sense that the ways in which we control these two actions also differ. In this chapter, you will be introduced to the two basic modes of control that we use when completing skilled movements such as those required in the "simple" skill of hammering a nail.

◼ ◼ ◼

In chapter 3, I mentioned that skill classification raises important issues regarding how we control our movements. In this chapter, I will discuss two basic modes of control that researchers believe are used to control our movements—continuous control and no-feedback control. Both modes of control rely on information that we receive from a variety of senses, so I will first discuss these sources of sensory information.

Sources of Sensory Information

For our purposes, I will discuss six basic sources of sensory information that we typically use to help us control our movements. Note that the order in which these topics are addressed here does not indicate their relative importance.

Observe, record, tabulate, communicate. Use your five senses. Learn to see, learn to hear, learn to feel, learn to smell, and know that by practice alone you can become expert.

William Osler

Vision

The first source of sensory information is vision, which we often use as our primary source of information. In fact, we tend to use visual information even when it is not the best source of information or is contradicted by other sensory information. For example, it is quite common to have the sensation that your car is rolling backward if you see the car in front of you moving forward through the periphery of your vision. This occurs despite the fact that you are also receiving very clear information that your foot is firmly on the brake pedal and that there is no vibration associated with the movement of your car.

In most cases, however, vision is a rich and accurate source of information about our environment, especially as it relates to movement. Vision gives us information about the paths along which we walk, run, cycle, and drive; the objects we manipulate such as scissors, pens, power drills, and cell phones; the targets we aim for when we play games such as soccer and darts or when we complete actions such as putting a key into a lock; and a wide variety of other features about the people, objects, and settings we interact with.

Hearing

The second source of sensory information is hearing. There are many examples to illustrate how our sense of hearing gives us information relevant to controlling our movements. Screeching tires or a horn can tell us of an impending collision with a car or motorcycle. The sound of contact between a golf ball and club or a baseball and bat tells us if we have hit the *sweet spot*. The starter's gun tells us when to begin a race. The sound of creaking floorboards can help guide our walking as we try not to wake a sleeping baby in our house. Of course, verbal communication between people is also used quite often to help us control our movements, for example when a music teacher tells a musician that a particular note was "too high" or "too low."

Balance

The third source of sensory information is derived from our sense of balance. If you try standing on one foot, you will notice that you gradually sway in one direction and then make a postural adjustment to bring yourself back to a more stable position. The information you use to make these corrections comes, in part, from your sense of balance. Because balance is a critical aspect of our capability to remain upright, it plays a role in virtually all of our actions involving standing or moving from one location to another (e.g., walking, running, and cycling). The sensory system that gives us information about balance can also tell us about the orientation of our body in space. Information about balance and orientation plays a central role in sports such as diving. For example, platform divers sometimes balance on their hands to start a dive and then complete several twists and flips as they descend toward the water.

TECHNOLOGY HIGHLIGHT

Visual Occlusion Techniques to Understand the Role of Vision

Although we often use information from a variety of sensory sources, it is sometimes helpful to isolate the role of individual senses to gain a better understanding of the extent to which they guide movement skills. Because vision is usually our dominant source of sensory information, researchers have developed many ways to explore how we use vision. One of these techniques is called visual occlusion. In this technique the researcher hides body parts or movements, often via video or film editing, in order to study how people use vision to anticipate the best course of action.

Suppose you want to know how an expert tennis player uses visual information to respond to an opponent's serve. One question that might emerge is whether or not experts are simply better at tracking the tennis ball than novices. On the other hand, it seems likely that experts learn to anticipate the serve because the speed at which the ball travels simply does not allow much time to respond. To test this proposal, you could show experts and novices a video clip of a service from a receiving player's perspective, but stop the clip at the moment of ball contact. If visually based anticipation does not distinguish between the experts and novices, they should be equally successful at predicting the location of the serve. If visual information preceding ball contact is used to anticipate the serve, you would expect the experts to have more accurate predictions, which is actually the case. To get an even clearer picture of how experts use visual information, you could stop the video clip at earlier and earlier points until you find that the predictions are no more accurate than chance. As it turns out, experts are better than novices at extracting information from visual cues related to the opponent's posture during the portions of the serve preceding ball contact (Williams et al., 2002, 2004).

Skill Insight

Our capability to balance decreases as we age. Richard Bohannon and his colleagues tested adults ranging from 20 to 79 years of age by asking them to stand on one foot with their eyes either open or closed (Bohannon et al., 1984). The results showed that the older participants did not balance as long as the younger participants, especially when they closed their eyes. This study provided important information to help physical therapists establish appropriate age-related expectations when implementing timed balance tests as a neurological assessment tool. The researchers also reported that the younger participants tried harder to stay balanced, which suggests that confidence may be an important factor to consider when one is teaching balance strategies to older people.

Touch

The fourth source of sensory information we use to control our movements is generated when we touch things. Touch conveys a wide range of information, including pressure, temperature, shape, texture, and vibration. A rock climber who feels for a solid handhold that he cannot see uses information from touch to determine both the shape and the texture of the handhold. A dentist uses information from touch to apply the appropriate amount of pressure when she drills out a cavity. If you ever take a ceramics class, you will learn that touch is very important when you are shaping clay on a potter's wheel.

Proprioception and Kinesthesis

The fifth and sixth sources of sensory information are closely related, so I will discuss them together. Both have to do with how we know about the positioning and movements of our limbs. **Proprioception** refers to information about the positions of our limbs. This information allows you to know the answer when you ask someone to guess how many fingers you are holding up behind your back. Anytime you have learned to reach for something without looking, you have used information from proprioception. Bartenders often use proprioception as they reach for bottles without looking. A bartender's "well" is set up in a standardized configuration to facilitate this type of behavior. Each bottle is always located in the same spot, so the bartender can find it easily while still interacting with the customer. You rely on proprioception every time you pick up a drink from the cup holder in your car.

Kinesthesis refers to information about the movement of our limbs. It gives us a general sense of how our limbs move in relation to one another as well as how fast our limbs are moving. Track coaches sometimes advise runners to synchronize their arm and leg movements, a technique that relies

proprioception—The source of sensory information that tells us about the positions of our limbs in space.

kinesthesis—The source of sensory information that tells us about the movements of our limbs in space.

Skill Insight

Even "simple" actions can be negatively influenced by a poorly designed user interface. Consider the case of placement of the control knobs on a stove (Proctor & Vu, 2006). On many stoves, the burners are arranged so that each one is closest to one of the four corners of the stove top. Unfortunately, control knobs are just as often arranged in a single horizontal row across either the front or the back of the stove. This arrangement makes it very hard to determine which knob controls which burner, so it is easy to turn on the wrong burner (and then wonder why it is taking so long for water to boil). In cases in which you have several burners on, you might turn the wrong one off, which will result in overcooking one dish and undercooking another. If you are under pressure to complete the meal in a certain time (e.g., if company is arriving soon for dinner), these types of errors can be extremely frustrating. This example is commonly used in human factors textbooks to illustrate that our environment influences the way we process information and that this processing, in turn, influences our performance.

heavily on kinesthesis. Other examples of kinesthesis include when you sense what it "feels" like to swing a golf club or tennis racket correctly, or how to move your feet to complete the steps of a dance sequence without looking. It is sometimes difficult to separate kinesthesis from proprioception, and I recommend that you just keep in mind that together they tell you about the positions and movements of your limbs.

Sensory Integration

Although I've just discussed six different sources of sensory information separately, it is important to recognize that they all work together in a tightly integrated system. Take the rock climbing example I used to illustrate how we acquire information from touch. When we look at the action of finding a handhold within a slightly larger context, we see that the climber uses many sources of sensory information and that some of them may actually overlap. The climber may first use vision to look at the general area as he moves his hand in search of a solid handhold. He is also receiving information from proprioception and kinesthesis during his reach. As his hand touches the rock face, he begins to feel around, using touch to locate a specific handhold. If he dislodges some loose debris, he will probably hear it as it breaks free. Meanwhile, he is using his sense of balance to make sure that he does not overextend his reach, thereby compromising the foothold that is currently supporting most of his weight. In learning to control any movement, the challenge we often face is learning to identify and use the most appropriate sources of sensory information (either alone or in combination).

Continuous Control

Continuous control (often called *closed-loop control*) is to a mode of controlling our movements in situations that allow us to use information resulting from our performance to make corrections (or decide that no correction is needed) while we are still engaged in the movement. In order for us to make these corrections, the skill must be slow and continuous so that we have enough time to process the information regarding our performance and then act on it before the movement ends. Because of the time it takes to complete the three stages of information processing that I discussed in the introduction to part II (stimulus identification, response selection, and response programming), it is generally accepted that we are capable of making no more than three corrections per second during continuous movements. Keeping a car in the middle of the lane while driving is a good example of how we use continuous control. As we move toward one side of the lane or the other, we use visual information regarding our relative position in the lane to steer the car back toward the center.

continuous control—A way of controlling slow continuous movements through the use of feedback generated by the movements to make corrections before the movements end; often referred to as closed-loop control because feedback information "loops" back to the performer during the movement.

When using continuous control, the performer generates an idea about a desired movement or movement outcome. She holds onto this idea while she assembles an action plan to tell her muscles how to contract to complete the desired movement. As the movement proceeds, she monitors sensory information that results from the movement and compares this to the idea she has for the desired movement. If they match, she continues her performance unchanged. If they do not match, she modifies the action plan she is using to alter her movements so that they more closely match the desired outcome. Suppose, for example, that you are using a power jigsaw to cut a line in a piece of wood (see figure 4.1). Your desired movement is to guide the saw so that the blade cuts along the marked line. As you move the saw, you will likely use vision to monitor how well you are doing. If you start to veer away from the line, you will correct yourself. If you have experience using a jigsaw, you will also use proprioception and kinesthesis to monitor your arm and hand position because if you let the saw get too far ahead of you, it is easier to let it pull to one side or the other.

There are many other examples of how we use various sources of sensory information to control our movements in a continuous fashion. An auto mechanic who needs to thread a nut onto a bolt will use vision and touch to align the nut properly. In cases in

© Natali_ua/Fotolia.com

FIGURE 4.1 Using a jigsaw requires continuous control in that the person uses information resulting from the performance to make corrections while still sawing the same line.

which she cannot see the bolt, she may instead rely on proprioception and touch. A musician or singer relies on hearing when he practices holding a note for an extended period of time. Deviations from the desired sound signal him to correct his performance. In the example of standing on one foot that I discussed earlier, you use information from vision, the pressure on the sole of your foot, movements in your ankle, and your sense of balance to detect when you are moving "out of balance" and then you implement corrective action to prevent a fall.

In the fields of observation, chance favors only the prepared mind.

Louis Pasteur

No-Feedback Control

One of the limitations of the continuous mode of control is that the amount of time it takes to process information can sometimes be relatively long compared to the duration of the movement. Many movements happen so quickly that they simply don't allow us to make corrections before they are over. For example, in the study of the surfing takeoff I mentioned in chapter 3, we discovered that the transition to the standing phase of the maneuver took as little as .15 seconds, which is about half the amount of time to make a single correction using continuous control. When we need to complete rapid movements, we use a **no-feedback control** mode, which allows us to preplan our movements so they can be carried out without correction.

No-feedback control is also known as *open-loop control* because the information created by the movement does not reach the performer in time to be used during the movement; thus the "loop" remains open. In preplanning a rapid discrete movement, we create what is called a **motor program,** a set of prestructured commands that specifies the pattern of movement to be completed. We still use sensory information in no-feedback control, but we use it before rather than during the movement. For example, we use vision to assess the distance we need to hit a golf ball and the direction in which we need to hit it. This is an example of assessing the conditions of the performance setting in order to identify movement goals and decide what types of movements will be likely to achieve those goals.

We also use information from one rapid movement as feedback to help us plan a subsequent rapid movement. For example, after a gymnast completes a forward flip on the balance beam, she receives information about the quality and result of her movement that she can then use in her attempts to improve subsequent performances. Suppose that she does not rotate fully and so needs to lean forward to maintain her balance. This information tells her something about how to

no-feedback control—A way of controlling rapid discrete movements through the use of information to plan the movement in advance and complete the action without benefit of feedback; often referred to as open-loop control because feedback information does not make it back around the "loop" (i.e., leaves it open) in time for the performer to use it during the movement.

motor program—A set of instructions compiled by our central nervous system in advance of a rapid movement and then sent to our muscles so that they execute the movement without the need for feedback during the action.

plan future attempts to ensure full rotation. She may need to rotate her arms more rapidly when initiating the flip, or she may need to tuck tighter to ensure that she rotates at an appropriate speed. Hitting a golf ball provides another good example of how we use sensory information from one rapid movement to plan future actions. When you hit the ball, you can see where it goes, hear whether or not you made solid contact, feel the motion of the club swing, feel the force and vibration caused by the contact, and feel if you are off balance (e.g., if you have to take a step during your follow-through). The next time you perform a golf swing, you will know to adjust your performance to prevent the mistakes you made the first time, or not to change anything if your first swing was acceptable.

SUCCESS STORY

Jill Whitall, University of Maryland (Baltimore)

Jill Whitall, PhD, began her path toward becoming a research professor as a physical education major in Cheshire, England. After teaching high school for a number of years, she returned to her studies to receive a master's degree in education from the University of London and a doctoral degree in motor development from the University of Maryland. She has held faculty positions at the University of Wisconsin, the University of Maryland (College Park), and the University of Maryland School of Medicine. Dr. Whitall is an active researcher, studying issues of motor development in both children and aging adults. In her research, she has examined the role of vision in grasping actions and the coordination of the limbs during walking in young children; she has also studied topics related to the rehabilitation of stroke patients. One of her most influen-

tial research studies (Whitall et al., 2000) demonstrated that a rehabilitation protocol involving bilateral arm training improved motor function in stroke patients and that this improvement was well maintained for several weeks. Prior to studies such as this one, stroke rehabilitation tended to focus either on just the affected limb or on helping the patient to learn how to rely only on the unaffected limb. Recently, Dr. Whitall was elected president of the North American Society for the Psychology of Sport and Physical Activity. She currently holds a faculty position in the Department of Physical Therapy and Rehabilitation Science at the University of Maryland (Baltimore).

Photo courtesy of Jill Whitall.

Combining Continuous and No-Feedback Control

Just as it is important to recognize that all of your senses are tightly integrated to provide you with information you can use to control your movements, it is important to recognize that many movements are accomplished through a combination of continuous and no-feedback control processes. For example, when threading a needle, you will likely use continuous control to guide the thread through the hole. Once the needle is threaded, you can use no-feedback control to rapidly pull more of the thread until you reach the desired length. The opening scenario for this chapter involved aspects of driving a nail that use continuous and no-feedback control (i.e., positioning the nail and then striking it, respectively). Similarly, driving a car involves many aspects that are controlled in different ways. Whereas maintaining your position in a lane uses continuous control, swerving rapidly to avoid hitting a squirrel uses no-feedback control.

It is also important to recognize that how you look at a movement skill might determine if you think it is being controlled in a continuous or a no-feedback fashion. When looking at a floor routine in gymnastics, you might see that the gymnast makes an error on one element that requires her to adjust her position so the next element does not take her off the mat. From this perspective, you could argue that this is an example of continuous control. However, when you consider how the gymnast controls most of the individual elements, you will see that they are rapid enough to require no-feedback control. As with many of the topics in motor behavior, our intent should not be to definitively say that this skill or that skill is controlled using one mode of control or the other. Rather, the goal is to consider how an action might be controlled so that we can better understand how the performer meets specific task demands in a given performance setting.

The Short of It

- We use information from several sources to help us control our movements. Although vision is often thought to be our dominant sense, we could not move effectively without also using balance, hearing, touch, and the information our body detects about the position and movements of our limbs in space (i.e., proprioception and kinesthesis).
- The term sensory integration refers to the fact that we typically use information from a variety of our senses any time we control our movements.
- There are two ways in which we control our movements. Continuous control allows us to use feedback to make corrections during slow continuous tasks. When we need to complete a rapid discrete action, we use no-feedback control to preplan our movement.

CHAPTER 5

Understanding How We Learn Motor Skills

✓ Many of the ways in which we learn motor skills, ranging from situations in which we are actually unaware of what we are learning to situations in which we purposefully engage in physical practice

✓ The basis for how practice on one skill or in one setting can benefit performance on another skill or in another setting

✓ How feedback affects performance and learning, and why too much feedback undermines learning

> If people knew how hard I worked to get my mastery, it wouldn't seem so wonderful at all.
>
> **Michelangelo Buonarroti**

Just off Highway 1 in central California, there are several small coves on the Pacific Ocean that serve as the local arena for a handful of highly skilled surfers. Most of these surfers are not the ones you will see in magazines or movies. For them, surfing is a lifestyle, and their participation in the sport is driven by their passion to surf. One characteristic of most skilled surfers that can be readily observed is the amount of time they spend watching the ocean in general and the waves in particular. Part of the reason for this may be the indefinable allure of the ocean itself, but among the best surfers this viewing also serves an important function in their surfing skill. To become good, a surfer must learn to judge the waves and conditions of the specific location to be surfed. Experienced surfers often do this for a period of time before entering the water. They look for how the waves are approaching, where they are breaking, and how big they are, as well as other conditions such as currents or crowds. This helps the surfers understand where they need to position themselves to catch the best waves and what to do if they find themselves in a potential trouble spot. By viewing the waves and predicting when and how they will break, the surfers get practice in anticipating a critical aspect of the environment. If they watch other surfers, they can also learn what works and what doesn't at a particular spot on a given day.

Theories of How We Learn

Over the years, many different theories have been used to explain how people learn (Adams, 1971; Schmidt, 1975). Some of these theories have been attempts to explain learning in general while others have focused mainly on the learning of motor skills. Today, one idea has emerged as the most widely adopted view of motor learning. **Schema theory** (Schmidt, 1975) states that as we learn a motor skill, we develop a rule that shows the relationship between movement outcomes and things such as our intended goal, the conditions of the performance setting, and the details of the motor program created to control the movement.

Suppose you want to learn to play darts. Your intended goal is to throw the dart so that it lands in the bull's-eye. The conditions of the performance setting would include things such as the distance to the dart board and the lighting in the room. As you prepare to throw the dart, you will generate a motor program that specifies things such as the direction of the throw, the angle of release, and the force of the throw. Once you throw the dart, you will receive sensory information about how the throw felt and where the dart landed. If you do this often enough, you will learn a rule (i.e., you will develop a *schema*) that connects these aspects of the performance. To simplify this idea, just think about how hard you will need to throw the dart. Let's assume that because you are inexperienced, you aim right at the bull's-eye and throw the dart with very little arc. On your first try, the dart hits about 6 inches (15 centimeters) below the target. On your next attempt, you throw the dart a little bit harder and it lands about 2 inches (5 centimeters) low. On your third attempt, you throw the dart with even more force, and now it lands just below the bull's-eye.

> **schema theory**—A theory of motor learning stating that memories for motor skills are stored as a general rule about the relationships between the performer's goal, the conditions of the performance setting, and the outcome of closely related movements.

With enough practice, you will eventually develop a schema that relates throwing force to where the dart lands. That is, throws with less force allow the dart to fall to a lower position. Once you have learned this rule, you might find that aiming a little bit above your target will enable you to throw the dart with a comfortable force that will give it the appropriate arc to get to the board without falling too low.

In chapter 4, I discussed how no-feedback control requires the use of a motor program. A motor program is set of commands we create in our central nervous system that contains information about the pattern of muscle activation needed for a given movement (Schmidt, 1975; Schmidt & Lee, 2005; Schmidt & Wrisberg, 2008). The schema or rule, such as the one developed by the dart thrower, consists of flexible and adaptable motor programs (called *generalized motor programs*). These programs consist of two types of information. The first relates to the patterns of movement that do not change from performance to performance of very similar actions. An example is the way in which we complete an overhand throw. As we bring our throwing arm behind our head, we step forward with the foot on the opposite side of the body. While we are still stepping, we rapidly bring our arm forward, leading with the elbow. We then plant our stepping foot just before releasing the ball. These aspects define the overhand throw,

Skill Insight

Being able to see what you are doing doesn't always improve your performance. The idea that taking away a person's vision of a target will reduce aiming accuracy seems fairly straightforward. However, adding vision does not always improve accuracy. Luc Proteau and his colleagues have shown that adding vision in an aiming task that had been learned without vision actually reduced accuracy (Proteau, Marteniuk, & Lèvesque, 1992). This finding illustrates that the type of sensory information we use in controlling a movement is highly influenced by the information that was available to us as we learned the skill.

and so they don't change much from throw to throw. The second type of information relates to the aspects that we do change from throw to throw, such as the force, direction, and release point. We change these in order to throw to targets at different locations and distances. These changeable aspects of the motor program are what we specify during the response programming stage of information processing.

There are, of course, other explanations of how we learn motor skills, and you will learn about these if you decide to study motor behavior. One thing that almost all theories of learning emphasize is that practice is a critical element in developing proficiency in motor skills. Regardless of how we explain motor learning, we should always recognize the important role of practice. This may seem obvious, but if you listen carefully to the way people talk about movement skills such as those involved in sport or dance, you will probably notice that in the view of many, highly skilled people are simply born that way. Not only is this an incorrect notion (Ericsson, Krampe, & Tesch-Römer, 1993; Howe, Davidson, & Sloboda, 1998), it also takes credit away from the performer for the years of dedicated practice that he or she has engaged in to reach such a high level of skill.

Ways We Learn Motor Skills

Now that you have learned about the process of learning motor skills, I will introduce you to several of the different ways we learn skills.

Explicit and Implicit Learning

Most of the time when we learn motor skills in formal settings, we are given explicit instructions. A youth league soccer coach might tell his players that they need to lean back to kick a loft pass. A young girl might tell her little brother about the order in which he needs to hop through the boxes in the game of hopscotch. A personal trainer might instruct a client to keep his back flat while doing the bench press. These are examples of **explicit learning,** in which the learner is clearly aware that he or she is learning a skill. In many instances, however, we are not entirely aware that we are learning certain aspects of a motor skill (Magill, 1998). If you learned to ride a bicycle as a child, you probably focused your attention on balancing, steering to avoid obstacles, and pedaling, but you were probably not aware that you were learning to shift your weight in the seat or that you applied more pressure to the pedals with your dominant foot. These aspects of performance that you learn without explicit awareness are the result of an **implicit learning** process. Often, we eventually become aware of some of the things we learn implicitly. For example, suppose that when you learned to ride a bike, you stuck your knees out to the side as you pedaled. Although this was not good technique, you learned this way, partly because you just weren't aware of what you were doing.

explicit learning—A type of learning in which the person is consciously aware of acquiring a skill.

implicit learning—A type of learning in which the person is not aware of acquiring a skill.

Chances are, however, that you eventually noticed this implicitly learned, incorrect technique and then *explicitly* tried to correct it.

Typing on a computer keyboard provides another good illustration of implicit learning. If you type frequently, you have undoubtedly implicitly learned certain keystroke patterns for frequently used letter combinations. If you are like me, you frequently type "teh" instead of "the" because you have implicitly learned the incorrect sequence of letters. This is such a common phenomenon that most word processing programs automatically correct it (which gives us little incentive to change the pattern even after we notice it). Another word that gets me is "performance," which I frequently type as "perfromance." Unfortunately, my software doesn't automatically change this one (it does, however, recognize it as an error, so I have no excuses if it is misspelled in this book). Incidentally, these two examples provide a good illustration of how human factors and usability professionals in the software industry have used their understanding of motor behavior to design systems that automatically compensate for common movement mistakes. Now, I hope you don't get the idea that implicit learning always leads to learning improper technique. There are also plenty of positive performance characteristics that you learn implicitly. To continue with the bike riding example, much of what you do to shift your weight will be learned implicitly. For example, you may learn to lean into turns and shift your weight rearward when you ride down a hill.

Physical Practice

As I mentioned earlier, physical practice is an essential component of the learning process. In fact, it is probably the single most effective way to learn motor skills. We often hear the adage "Practice makes perfect," but there are a couple of things wrong with this idea. First, how you practice must be given serious consideration. Putting in the time to improve a motor skill will not be very rewarding if you don't engage in the appropriate type of practice. Second, the process of learning is about making mistakes, not performing flawlessly. The notion of perfection is at odds with the reality that we actually learn from our mistakes.

 You can always become better.

Tiger Woods

There are several different ways in which you might engage in physical practice of motor skills. Often, instructors break a complex movement into smaller parts to make it more manageable for the learner (Christina & Corcos, 1988; Wrisberg, 2007). This technique is known as **part practice.** For example, a swimming instructor may teach a kicking technique separately from the arm stroke. Or new swimmers might hold on to the wall and kick, while more advanced swimmers could complete laps using a kickboard. Another example is seen when a pole vaulter practices her approach without actually planting the pole or vaulting. Part practice is also used to simplify a task by removing

part practice—A type of physical practice in which a skill is broken into parts to simplify the learning process.

FIGURE 5.1 Part practice involves breaking complex movements into smaller or simpler parts, such as when a ball is placed on a tee to allow the learner to focus only on the swinging motion.

an aspect of performance that is not necessarily a part of the movement itself. For example, most kids learn to hit a baseball or softball by using a batting tee (figure 5.1). The use of the tee does not take any parts away from the movement of the swing, but it reduces the performance demand associated with tracking a moving ball and timing the swing correctly. With these demands eliminated, the learner can focus on swinging the bat correctly so that it hits the ball. An important consideration in deciding to use part practice techniques is whether breaking the skill into parts will alter the fundamental pattern of movement. Some swimming instructors do not use part practice because they believe that the coordination of upper and lower body movements is an important element of swimming that can be learned only through practice of the whole task.

Physical practice can also be accomplished using simulators. A simulator is any device aimed at reproducing the conditions under which a task is normally performed. Only the most sophisticated devices can actually come close to replicating reality. Among these simulators are the ones used by race car drivers (see figure 5.2), astronauts, and commercial or military pilots. Most other simulators are designed to replicate critical aspects related to task demands and performance settings. A pitching machine, for example, does a great job of replicating the demand of hitting a rapidly approaching baseball or softball. As virtual reality technology becomes more and more sophisticated, simulators will become extremely lifelike and will probably provide a realistic option for training an increasing number of skills. One of the major drawbacks of these types of devices is that they tend to be expensive, so access to them is quite limited. It is also important to keep in mind that some simulators are made strictly for entertainment and may not be useful training devices.

Mental Practice and Imagery

We can also practice motor skills using mental practice and mental imagery techniques that require no physical movements (Feltz & Landers, 1983; Wrisberg, 2007). In its simplest form, **mental practice** refers to mentally rehearsing the procedural elements of a skill. For example, you should have no problem mentally picturing

Photo courtesy of Motorsport Simulators, LLC.

FIGURE 5.2   A simulator designed to train race car drivers.

the steps you would go through to call your best friend on the phone. The sequence may involve picking up your cell phone and pressing the button to activate your address list. Then you would press the button to scroll down to your friend's name, select it, and press the button to start the call. The procedures for your particular phone might be a little bit different, but you probably get the idea. Another technique is called **mental imagery,** in which the learner imagines herself performing the motor skill, focusing on as many sources of sensory information as possible. In this case for the phone example, not only would you see yourself operating the cell phone, you would also try to re-create in your mind the associated sounds, information from touch, and the feelings you might have in the moment (e.g., you may image yourself as anxious and dialing as fast as possible).

> **mental practice**—A type of practice that involves mentally rehearsing the steps involved in the actual execution of a motor skill.
>
> **mental imagery**—A type of practice that involves attempting to create a mental image of as many aspects of a performance as possible, including both the steps involved in a motor skill and what it feels like to complete the skill.

Mental practice and imagery have many potential benefits. They can be combined with physical practice. They can be used when physical practice is either not possible (e.g., when someone is injured or is traveling) or too fatiguing (e.g., if the learner has a medical condition that limits the amount of physical work he or she can perform), or when opportunities to practice are limited by the nature of the task (e.g., downhill ski racing). Mental practice and imagery can be used to practice decision-making aspects of skills, the identification of task-relevant cues, and the management of arousal. The fact that mental imagery can evoke physical changes is readily illustrated by the following example, adapted from another popular textbook on motor behavior (Schmidt & Wrisberg, 2008). Imagine that you walk into

Skill Insight

Studies have shown that children as young as 3 years old are very good at recognizing the movements of humans and animals by watching motion cues. These cues are points of white light on a dark background that represent segments of the body as it moves. Some of these "point-light display" studies have used as few as 13 points to represent fairly complex movements such as walking or a karate kick. Marina Pavlova and her colleagues asked children and adults to view moving point-light displays showing either a person, a dog, or a bird walking (Pavlova et al., 2001). Both children and adults were able to identify the person or animal in the moving displays. Interestingly, however, they could not do this based on a static picture of the same points. Studies such as this one illustrate that humans can extract useful information about people and animals just by detecting the relative motion of their parts. This may represent one of our biologically "built-in" features that enable us to easily (in most cases) navigate such complex and constantly changing settings as a crowded airport.

your kitchen and see a big yellow lemon on the cutting board. Pay attention to all the details. Are there dishes in the sink? Are the blinds open or closed? You walk across the kitchen and stand at the counter. You pick up the knife and carefully cut the lemon in half. Now, you pick up half the lemon, tilt your head back, and open your mouth. You slowly squeeze the lemon and a drop of juice falls onto your tongue. If you are like most people, your mouth actually watered when you read this, which illustrates the power of the mind to induce physical changes in the body. Mental practice and imagery may not be as powerful as physical practice, but their benefits have been demonstrated enough times that we should view them as effective tools, among many others, for learning motor skills.

Observational Learning

Another common way we learn skills is by imitating the actions of another person. This technique is usually referred to as **observational learning** or *modeling* (McCullagh, 1986, 1987). As a child, you probably learned to mimic the facial expressions of your parents through observation. It is also likely that you have used observational learning extensively throughout your life to learn various aspects of movement-related activities. Young children often learn aspects of common childhood movement activities by watching others (e.g., skipping, jumping rope, or kicking a ball). In many cases, your observations supported more explicit instruction and physical practice. For example, a parent, coach, or teacher probably taught you how to kick a ball at some point, but it is also quite likely that you learned certain aspects of the skill by watching your peers (e.g., to lengthen your approach when you want to kick the ball farther).

observational learning—A type of practice in which a learner watches the performance of another person modeling a skill. The model can be either a skilled performer or another learner. Observation is often accomplished through the use of recorded demonstrations.

Recent research in neuroscience has identified the presence of "mirror neurons" that are thought to play a large role in our capability to imitate others (Rizolatti & Craighero, 2004). These neurons are activated both when we perform an action and when we only observe the action. The identification of these neurons suggests that we are biologically predisposed to learn through observation.

The best and fastest way to learn a sport is to watch and imitate a champion.

Jean-Claude Killy

Through observation, we can learn about movement strategies and gather information regarding patterns of coordination. Movement strategies might sometimes be considered "tricks" to help us perform, for example when a baseball player learns to field ground balls by first moving his glove to the ground and then lifting it up to the ball if needed. The patterns of coordination of a movement refer to spatial information such as the relative positioning of our limbs and the timing of our movements (e.g., when we jump from the left foot at the same time we reach with the right arm during a layup).

Trial and Error

In many cases, we learn motor skills through extensive **trial and error.** For example, athletes in sports such as skateboarding, surfing, and snowboarding have learned to execute incredibly complex maneuvers despite a lack of formal coaching. Many people also reach a relatively high level of proficiency in activities such as dance, pottery, and painting through trial-and-error learning. This, of course, does not mean that this is the preferred way of learning. Instructors and coaches are typically needed in order for people to reach the highest levels of performance, or at least to expedite the learning process. Another concern related to trial-and-error learning is that it can lead to learning what we might call "bad habits" (e.g., ineffective patterns of coordination), which might limit the ultimate level of proficiency we achieve. We often engage in trial-and-error learning to optimize movements related to some routine aspect of our lives. For example, you may have found yourself trying different techniques to more quickly type text messages (e.g., using two thumbs or multiple fingers) on your cell phone. This does not mean, however, that the technique you discovered is actually the best one in the long run even if it did speed up your texting when you first tried it.

trial and error—A type of learning in which a person tries a variety of approaches to learning a motor skill and evaluates their effectiveness based on his or her own personal experience with each approach.

Using a systematic approach to compare a variety of techniques as employed by a relatively large number of people is the recommended way to discover the best techniques. So, while trial-and-error learning may have its place, it certainly does not represent the best approach when you truly want to learn to perform at the highest level you can. Interestingly, though, trial-and-error learning may play a role in establishing a foundation for future skill learning. Research on the development of expertise in sport has shown that elite athletes typically engage in a wide variety of sports during what are known as the "sampling years" from around 6 to 12 years of age (Côté, 1999). Some argue that this provides the athlete with a solid base of fundamental motor skills (e.g., running, jumping, throwing, and catching) upon which later specialized training can build. Because activities during the sampling years are under the control of the learner, it is also possible that this sense of control might increase motivation to continue practicing (Deci & Ryan, 1985).

Transfer

The different ways of learning motor skills I have just described should not be considered independent of one another. In any motor skill learning experience, it is likely that the performer will learn various aspects of the skill in different ways or work on the same aspect in different ways at different times over the course of learning. It is a good idea to think of these different ways in which we learn motor skills as tools that we have available to us to enhance both the learning experience and the ultimate level of skill resulting from that experience. For example, I learned to surf by physically practicing, observing my peers, and engaging in a lot of trial and error. When I first started, I also used quite a bit of part practice because I would tend to fall as soon as I caught the wave and so was practicing only the first part of the takeoff maneuver.

Remember that one of the themes of this book is that we need to account for the various dimensions of the person, task, and performance setting that influence motor performance and motor learning. In thinking about the performance setting, we should always recognize that the settings we practice our skills in will often differ from the settings in which we will eventually perform those skills. Imagine, for example, that you often ride your mountain bike on a trail near your home in an effort to improve your bike-handling skills (e.g., hopping the bike over logs or other obstacles). If you are successful, you will be able to use the skills you developed in one setting (the trails near your home) when you ride your bike in another setting (e.g., on new trails). The concept that what you learn in one performance setting can be adapted to another setting is called *transfer* (Adams, 1987; Hendrickson & Schroeder, 1941; Schmidt & Wrisberg, 2008). Transfer is the goal of most real-world motor learning because performance settings often change. Even that familiar trail you ride so often will change over time. New logs will fall, mud puddles will dry out or get bigger, and holes will move slightly or change their shapes.

In rehabilitation settings, transfer is the idea that therapy conducted in the clinic will prepare patients to function normally (or as close to normally as possible) once they return to their regular daily routines. Imagine, for example, a physical therapist working with an older person who has broken a hip. In the clinic, this patient will need to practice walking in ways that reflect the demands imposed by the real world. When the time is right, the physical therapist might ask her to complete skills such as walking up and down stairs, walking without crutches, walking around obstacles, and rising from a chair to walk across the room. All of these tasks are designed to enhance transfer.

Coaches also rely heavily on the concept of transfer. In fact, the whole idea of practice is based on the concept of transfer. Athletes perform their skills during practice with the goal of transferring these skills successfully to the playing field. The effectiveness of a practice session (and of the coach who designs it) is measured largely by how well it prepares athletes to compete. This, of course, is also true of any of the many professions that involve teaching people motor skills. Instructional settings should always be designed to facilitate transfer to the setting in which the skills will ultimately be performed, whether that is in recreational sport, dance, art, industry, or medicine.

Feedback

No discussion of how we learn motor skills is complete without some consideration of feedback. Feedback is a fundamental component of the learning process (Adams, 1978; Magill, 2007; Schmidt & Wrisberg, 2008). There are two general types of feedback, inherent and augmented. Inherent feedback is the information that is normally available to you as a result of engaging in a task. A good example of this type of feedback is when you can see the outcome of your actions in skills such as a basketball free throw or a golf putt. Other examples include hearing a baseball hit the "sweet spot" on a bat, feeling the wall of the swimming pool on your feet as you complete a flip turn, and falling off a balance beam during a gymnastics routine.

In chapter 4, I discussed the many sources of sensory information that we use to control our movements. Much of this information is often available as inherent feedback as well. It is important to distinguish feedback from information in general, however. For example, the sound of the starter's pistol in a 400-meter race is an example of sensory information that you use in this activity, but it is not feedback because it does not occur as a result of your actions. You might, however, incorporate this information to help make some inherent feedback more relevant, as when you think about the delay between hearing the pistol and other sensory information related to your start (e.g., pressure on your feet). You might use this comparison to recognize the quality of your start, which would be an example of inherent feedback.

Augmented feedback is information about your performance that you cannot obtain by yourself. Instead, you need another person or a device to provide this information. Examples include split times from a wristwatch, verbal feedback from a coach about diving technique, and the number on a speedometer indicating the effect of pressing on the accelerator. Augmented feedback is usually visual or verbal, but it can sometimes be conveyed using other sources of sensory information. For example, a football coach may nudge a lineman's foot to indicate that it is not placed in the correct position during a three-point stance, or a dance teacher may apply pressure to some part of the student's body (depending upon the type of dance) to indicate that she is moving in the wrong direction or is not moving fast enough (figure 5.3).

Augmented feedback may focus on either the outcome of the skill or the technique used during the skill. Although many activities are measured by the outcomes or results achieved, this information is often available as inherent feedback. For example, you don't need someone to tell you that you fell down when attempting a cartwheel. In other cases, outcomes are not readily apparent. One example is when a golfer hits a shot to an elevated green so that she cannot see where the ball comes to rest. If she is playing in a tournament and the ball lands close to the hole or runs off the green, the crowd's cheers or groans will give her some augmented feedback about the general outcome of her shot. Another example occurs when a surgeon is operating. In many instances, the surgeon cannot adequately gauge the patient's blood loss resulting from incisions, so he relies on instruments that measure blood pressure and heart rate as well as on support staff who monitor how much fluid has been transfused into the patient.

Information about the form or technique used in executing a motor skill is often not available to performers as inherent feedback, so they must rely on augmented feedback from an outside source. Feedback of this type most often comes from instructors or coaches who use their expertise to filter and interpret the information that is then relayed back to the performer. It might also come from measurement devices such as video cameras that can capture information about the pattern of movement. In some cases, inherent feedback is available but the performer needs help in learning to interpret it and uses augmented feedback to do so. This commonly occurs as we develop a "feel" for a correct technique. When we first begin to learn a skill, a coach or instructor can help us understand what our inherent feedback means. For example, if you frequently lose your balance when swinging a golf club, an instructor might tell that you are moving too quickly through the swing (a common problem). Once you learn this, you can use the inherent feedback related to your sense of balance to evaluate this aspect of the swing for yourself. This is not to say that augmented information is no longer helpful. Even great golfers such as Tiger Woods have swing coaches to provide them with information about the swing that they cannot readily access on their own.

© Roy Morsch/age fotostock

FIGURE 5.3 Dance instructors provide augmented feedback to help students learn correct body positions.

SUCCESS STORY

Pat Summitt, University of Tennessee Women's Basketball Coach

Pat Summitt began her journey toward becoming a basketball coach as a physical education major and basketball player at the University of Tennessee, Martin. After graduation, she moved to the University of Tennessee, Knoxville, to pursue a master's degree in physical education and work as an assistant coach. However, upon arriving in Knoxville, she was offered the position of head coach of the Lady Vols. In 35 years of coaching, she has accumulated an impressive number of wins (over 1,000) and eight national championships.

Summitt is famous for her competitive intensity; her players refer to "the look" to indicate the way Summitt can remind them to stay focused without saying a word. Despite her reputation for intensity, Summitt considers herself to be a teacher, a fact that is revealed by a close look at the way she prepares her teams. She has said that she considers practice to be a classroom and that she wants to help her players become "A" students by game time. When asked what her greatest strength is, she responded that it is her teaching skill. During practice, she prepares her players in ways that consistently reflect many of the principles of motor behavior. She provides them with instructions on how to execute movement skills and focus their attention appropriately. She acknowledges the capabilities and limitations that each player has and tailors her instruction accordingly. She encourages her players to evaluate their own performances and provides them with specific feedback when they need it. Finally, she tests her players' readiness by challenging them with many of the demands they will face during actual games (Alexander, 2009; SportSouth, 2009; UT Ladyvols.com, n.d.).

UT Lady Vol Media Relations.

When providing augmented feedback, whether it is about an outcome or technique, it is a good idea to keep in mind five "rules of thumb."

1. More is not always better. In fact, giving feedback too often can make a learner dependent upon the information provided to such an extent that performance actually suffers when the feedback is removed. Remember that the goal of most learning situations is to be able to transfer your skills to a different performance setting and that this new setting will often not provide instructional support such as feedback. Consequently, providing feedback too often can hinder the learner's capability to do the very thing that he or she is trying to do—perform the motor skill on his or her own. Research suggests that providing feedback after every fifth attempt is a good place to start (Schmidt, Lange, & Young, 1990). For new learners or difficult tasks, you might give feedback more frequently during initial practice. When feedback is given, it might provide information about only the last attempt, each of the previous attempts, or an average of each of the previous attempts.

2. Feedback should provide information about how to fix the problem when learners do not know how to correct their own errors. For example, a coach might tell a diver, "You didn't rotate enough on that dive; next time tuck tighter;" a therapist might tell a knee replacement patient, "Try to flex your knee more when your right leg accepts weight during walking." These feedback examples include information about how to increase the diver's speed of rotation (i.e., tuck tighter) and the knee replacement patient's knee flexion. For experienced performers, providing too much information of this sort might become a distraction if they already know how to fix their errors. They may need only feedback describing the outcome or form of the movement they are practicing (e.g., "Your splash was too big").

 Have you noticed that whatever sport you're trying to learn, some earnest person is always telling you to keep your knees bent?

Dave Barry

3. Delay feedback long enough for the learner to process her own inherent feedback. Giving feedback too quickly can interfere with this processing and impede the learner's efforts to develop her capability to evaluate her own performance. For a long time, it was thought that feedback should be given immediately after the completion of a motor skill, but research has shown that doing this actually interferes with learning (Swinnen et al., 1990). Instead, it is a good idea to let learners think about the movement on their own before giving them any feedback.

4. Have the learner estimate his own errors before feedback is provided. Rule 3 says that you should delay feedback long enough for the learner to self-evaluate his or her performance. A way of actually formalizing this process into practice is to explicitly ask learners to identify their errors during the delay between completing an attempt and receiving augmented feedback. Combining rules 3 and 4 will help ensure that learners develop the capability to detect and correct their own errors to the extent that this is possible. This will ultimately facilitate learners' independence from the instructional support provided during practice and allow them to transfer their skills to the desired performance setting.

5. Feedback should target aspects of the performance that the learner can control. Feedback should convey information about specific aspects of the performance that the learner can actually change. It will not help learners to tell them about a

TECHNOLOGY HIGHLIGHT

The Engagement Skills Trainer 2000

The Engagement Skills Trainer 2000 (EST 2000) is a virtual marksmanship training tool used primarily by army and national guard units in several countries. The EST 2000 is a portable simulator that authentically re-creates the demands of firing several different small-arms weapons. It consists of a projector, computer, and weapons connected to an air compressor. The computer allows the operator to configure a wide range of scenarios. For example, different types of firing ranges can be projected onto the screen, and the location and distance of targets can be manipulated. The weapons replicate actual weapons with respect to size and weight. Recoil and the sound of gunfire are created through the use of compressed air and a high-fidelity sound system, respectively. The system requires the trainee to follow standard firing range procedures that are used in training with live ammunition. Various aspects of marksmanship can be recorded such as the location where the weapon is aimed before and after the shot (used to examine stability of the aiming process), the location of the shot, and the time of trigger pull.

Recently, I have been involved in a project that uses an EST 2000 located at the United States Army Research Institute for Environmental Medicine in Natick, Massachusetts. We are examining the effects of self-controlled feedback (that is, allowing learners to decide if they would receive feedback after a trial) on marksmanship training in skilled military personnel and unskilled civilians. The EST 2000 gives precise control over the

performance demands we place on the participants and allows us to measure the aiming process as well as the outcome of the shots. Because the EST 2000 so closely resembles real-world demands, the results of this research are likely to be immediately relevant to army training procedures. For example, our results may lead to a recommendation to incorporate some level of self-control into existing training procedures.

Photos courtesy of Cubic Corporation Defense and Security Group.

The EST 2000 allows soldiers to train with a full suite of simulated weapons against realistic targets in current operating environments.

mistake that they cannot change. For example, a patient working on rehabilitating her shoulder may not have the strength to complete certain exercises with correct form. A skilled therapist would not ask her to complete these exercises and then tell her that her form was incorrect. Instead, the therapist will select an exercise that is more appropriate for the current capability of the patient.

The Short of It

- We can learn motor skills in a variety of different ways using both physical and mental practice techniques. Sometimes we are not even consciously aware of the skills we learn.

- All types of motor skill practice have the common goal of preparing learners to transfer their skills to performance situations that actually occur in real-world performance settings. The physical educator wants her students to be able to transfer fundamental motor skills or sport skills to actual participation in lifetime physical activities. The therapist wants his patients to transfer skills learned in the clinic to everyday functioning. Coaches want their athletes to transfer skills learned in practice to performance during games.

- Other than practice itself, feedback is one of the most influential factors in helping a learner to master a motor skill. The following are the five basic rules of feedback:

  1. Don't give it too often.

  2. Be sure it includes information about how to make corrections if the learner needs this.

  3. Delay it long enough after an attempt to allow the learner to process the experience.

  4. Before delivering it, ask the learner to estimate his or her own errors.

  5. Be sure that feedback focuses on specific aspects of the skill that the learner can control.

CHAPTER 6

Capabilities and Limitations

© Michael Pettigrew/Fotolia.com

✓ How we process information from the environment to make decisions and control our movements

✓ How anticipation and practice help us to respond faster

✓ How the limits of our attention influence motor performance and how directing our attention to specific aspects of our performance benefits performance

✓ How arousal affects performance

✓ The ways in which we must trade between speed and accuracy when completing certain movements

✓ Why it is important to recognize the differences between abilities and skills

> Fast is
> fine, but accuracy is
> everything.
>
> **Wyatt Earp**

Imagine you are driving your car to school. As you leave your neighborhood, you stop at a stop sign before turning right onto a busy street. Traffic is even heavier than normal, but you still notice the businesses along the side of the street. The coffee shop where you normally buy a cup of coffee reminds you that you are running late. The dry cleaner reminds you that you need to pick up your laundry on the way home. The red car in the other lane just in front of you has a big dent in the fender just like your neighbor's car. After driving a few blocks, you approach a busy intersection, and the light turns from green to yellow. What do you do? Do you brake, continue at the same speed, or perhaps even accelerate? Your decision will depend upon a wide variety of information you gather from the environment in addition to the message sent by the traffic signal. For example, you will probably base your decision on factors such as how fast you are traveling, how close you are to the intersection, and whether or not the car behind you is following you very closely. All of these factors can influence not only what your decision will be, but also how long it takes you to make it. When time is limited, even slight delays in preparing a response can lead to substantial problems in performance.

Now that you have learned a bit about how movements are controlled (chapter 4) and the ways we learn motor skills (chapter 5), it will be helpful to understand some of our basic capabilities and limitations that influence how well we can meet the various task demands we face when performing motor skills. I will begin by discussing some basic features of how humans process information to make decisions and prepare their movements. Then I will focus on issues related to the ways in which our attentional capacity and memory influence performance and learning. Finally, I will discuss speed–accuracy trade-offs and the distinction between abilities and skills.

Information Processing

In the introduction to part II, I brought up the idea that humans use information from the environment to guide their actions (Schmidt & Lee, 2005; Schmidt & Wrisberg, 2008). This can be seen as a tremendous capability because it allows us to be responsive to changing features of the environment so that we can adapt our actions accordingly. On the other hand, we do have some limitations in the ways we can process information, and these can sometimes negatively affect our performance.

Three Stages of Information Processing

The **information processing** perspective argues that we detect information from signals in our environment, use this information to decide how to act, and then prepare to act accordingly. In the opening scenario for this chapter, I related a common experience for most drivers. As we approach an intersection, the traffic light may change from green to yellow. In this example, seeing the light is the first of three steps we complete in information processing. Once we see the light, we use information stored in memory telling us that the yellow light serves as a warning: A red light will follow shortly, indicating that we cannot legally cross the intersection. When we see the yellow light, we need to make a decision about how to respond. This is the second step of information processing. The most common choices we have in this example include braking, maintaining our speed, or accelerating. Each of these calls for a different action to be executed: move the foot to the brake, keep the foot where it is, or depress the accelerator. Once we decide on the appropriate action, we need to prepare to implement it. This is the final step of information processing.

As you can see in figure 6.1, the three stages of information processing can be represented in a fairly simple model that indicates the sequence of events that occur when we process information from the environment to make decisions and prepare movements. All three stages are completed within a period of time known as *reaction time,* which is the amount of time it takes to begin to respond to a signal you cannot anticipate. So, the model essentially indicates what we have to do in order to act on new information.

The first stage of information processing is known as **stimulus identification.** It is during this stage that we recognize relevant information in our environment. This information can come from any one of the many sources of sensory information I discussed in chapter 4. We use vision to identify people and objects and to track motion. For example, when driving, we use vision to see pedestrians and traffic lights, the movement of our car relative to other objects that are either moving (e.g., cars) or stationary (e.g., road signs), hazards in the road (e.g., potholes), and our car's instrument panel. We use hearing to detect honking horns, screeching tires, and seat-belt or low-fuel warnings. We use other sources of sensory information

information processing—The stages humans go through when using information from the environment to plan and control their movements; information processing is generally considered to include at least three stages related to identifying cues, making decisions, and preparing the body to respond.

stimulus identification—The stage of information processing during which we detect information from the environment.

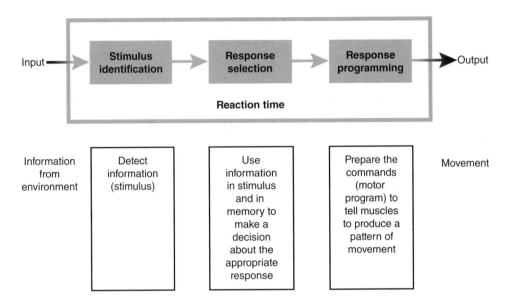

FIGURE 6.1 **A three-stage model of information processing. The stages include stimulus identification, response selection, and response programming. All three stages occur within the interval of time known as reaction time.**

Adapted, by permission, from R. Schmidt and C. Wrisberg, 2007, *Motor learning and performance*, 4th ed. (Champaign, IL: Human Kinetics), 30.

(e.g., touch, proprioception, and kinesthesis) to detect information related to vibration, how hard we press on the brake or accelerator, and where our hands and feet are in relation to the controls we operate while driving.

 Golf is recognized as one of the more difficult games to play or teach. One reason for this is that each person necessarily plays by feel, and a feel is almost impossible to describe.

Bobby Jones

The second stage of information processing is known as **response selection.** This is the stage when we make decisions based on the information we have detected during the previous stage. You will remember from chapter 3 that decision making is particularly important for *open skills,* which are performed in unpredictable environments. Once the information we receive from the environment reaches our attention, we compare it to other information we have stored in memory so that we can make an appropriate decision. We must have some knowledge of the ways in which the information is relevant within the context of our performance to be able to use the information effectively. This point was illustrated in a movie from the 1980s called *Starman.* In the movie, an

response selection—The stage of information processing during which we decide between possible responses to information we have gathered during stimulus identification.

alien "figures out" what he thinks are the appropriate responses to traffic signals by watching his human traveling companion drive her car: "Red light, stop. Green light, go. Yellow light, go very fast." Although this "rule" fits many of his observations, he clearly lacks the knowledge to ensure a correct decision when faced with a yellow light because he has no memories that allow him to understand that the context can change the way we act on a stimulus (in this case, the yellow light).

The third stage of information processing is known as **response programming.** During this stage, we put together commands to send to the muscles that will produce our intended movement response. In chapter 5, I described the idea of a *motor program,* which is a set of commands that tells muscles how to contract in a certain pattern to produce a specific coordinated movement. It may be helpful to think of the decision we make in the response selection stage as a choice of which motor program we will implement. The program contains information about the sequence and relative timing of the movements; but once it is selected, we still need to specify other aspects of the movement such as which limbs to use and how long the movement should last. Imagine, for example, that as you approach the intersection in the opening scenario you decide that your best choice is to accelerate through the intersection because the person behind you is following closely and does not seem to be paying attention. Imagine also that your car has a manual transmission that will require you to downshift so that you can accelerate rapidly enough to get through the intersection in time. You will select a motor program that specifies the sequence and timing of your movements to control the clutch, shift knob, and accelerator in a coordinated fashion. During response programming, you will also specify that this action is to be completed very rapidly because you have less time than usual to downshift.

Remember that this model is based on the assumption that we *react* to new information from the environment. In many activities, the amount of time we have to respond is limited, so a shorter **reaction time** (i.e., the time to complete the three stages of information processing) is advantageous. In chapter 3, you learned about *open skills,* which are those that take place in an unpredictable environment. I noted that open skills emphasize decision-making demands because the performer is reacting to new information from the environment. Another important point to consider is that there is usually some pressure to respond quickly in these situations because the unpredictability is often linked to movement in the environment. In other words, as changes unfold, the performer has a limited window of time to respond. Therefore, the faster she can identify the stimulus, select the response, and then program the response, the more time there will be to complete the necessary action.

> **response programming**—The stage of information processing during which we prepare our body to complete the action chosen during response selection.
>
> **reaction time**—The time it takes to complete all three stages of information processing when we must respond to unexpected information from the environment.

Factors That Influence Information Processing

There are several factors that influence each stage of information processing and can either speed up or slow down reaction time. These influences are summarized in table 6.1. The stimulus identification stage is influenced by the intensity of each stimulus as well as the number of possible stimuli. We typically react faster to more intense stimuli and more slowly to less intense stimuli. At the start of a sprint race, we react faster to a loud starter's pistol than to a soft verbal command to "go." In reading an instrument panel to control a vehicle or a piece of machinery, we react faster to displays that are brightly lit than to those that are dim (Proctor & Dutta, 1995). Stimulus identification is also influenced by the total number of possible cues in the environment, with more time needed for more cues (Hick, 1952). Imagine a soccer player bringing the ball downfield. In one scenario, he faces a single defender and so needs to monitor only the movement cues this defender sends. Consider another case in which the player instead faces three defenders. It will take longer to complete stimulus identification in this second case because the player must monitor a larger number of cues generated by three players. This will tend to slow reaction time and increase the likelihood that the player will respond too slowly to an attack.

The response selection stage is influenced by both the number of choices that can be made and the probability that a given choice is the correct one. When faced with more possible response choices, it takes longer to complete response selection (Hick, 1952; Hyman, 1953). The opening scenario indicates that the most likely choices a driver has when seeing a yellow light are to brake, accelerate, or maintain speed. It turns out that having to select from three choices will actually slow down our reaction time compared to the situation in which we have to choose between only two alternatives. Each time the number of response choices increases, the amount of time to complete response selection also increases. More complex environments typically afford more choices, but this can be a problem when only one choice is appropriate because the presence of so many alternatives slows down our reaction time.

Response selection is also affected by the probability that a given choice is a correct one. The less likely a response choice is, the longer it takes to react to its cue. We have all experienced this when we have been "caught off guard" and failed to respond appropriately to an environmental cue. If you play table tennis against

TABLE 6.1 Some Factors That Influence the Stages of Information Processing and Reaction Time

Stage	Factor	Influence on stage
Stimulus identification	Intensity of the stimulus (e.g., loudness)	Less intense stimuli require more time to be identified.
	Number of stimuli	Increasing the number of possible stimuli increases the amount of time required to identify the relevant stimulus.
Response selection	Number of response choices	Increasing the number of response choices increases the time required to select the response.
	Probability of a response choice	Less probable response choices require more time for response selection.
Response programming	Complexity of movement	More complex movements require more time for programming the response.

someone who has three strong serves but uses only two of them most of the time, you would be smart to expect one of the two more frequent serves. When she uses the third serve, however, you will be slower to react (assuming you were not able to detect the serve in advance). This gives her an advantage when using that particular serve, but she will keep that advantage only if she "saves" the serve. If she starts using it more often, you will learn that it is more likely to occur and your reaction time will improve.

 SUCCESS STORY

Carolee Winstein, University of Southern California

Carolee Winstein, PhD, is a physical therapist and professor in the University of Southern California's (USC) Division of Biokinesiology and Physical Therapy. Her academic training includes a bachelor's degree in kinesiology and psychology from the University of California at Los Angeles (UCLA) and a master's degree in physical therapy from USC. She also earned a doctoral degree in kinesiology from UCLA, specializing in motor behavior.

Dr. Winstein's research is largely translational in nature. Because of her clinical training as a physical therapist and her academic training as a movement scientist, her work is at the intersection of movement science and rehabilitation medicine. She focuses largely on issues related to rehabilitation following various neurological impairments such as those that result from stroke and Parkinson's disease. In some of her research, she uses a variety of new technologies to assess brain function while participants engage in functional movement tasks. Her laboratory at USC works to address three important aspects of neurorehabilitation. First, they conduct basic research to identify fundamental control and learning problems that apply to patients with various movement disorders. Second, they take these discoveries and test their potential clinical application by comparing them to standard rehabilitation approaches. Third, they provide the rehabilitation community as a whole with opportunities to engage in the developmental steps to generate evidence through clinical research that ranges from small preclinical trials to large-scale multisite clinical trials to evaluate the usefulness of specific rehabilitation interventions. For example, Dr. Winstein was colead investigator on a project that enlisted over 200 participants at seven different sites nationally to test the effectiveness of an intervention called constraint-induced movement therapy for the rehabilitation of arm function in stroke victims. This therapy restricts the use of the unaffected arm so that the patient works toward recovering the function of the impaired arm (Wolf et al., 2006).

Photo courtesy of Carolee Winstein.

The response programming stage is influenced by the complexity of the movement used in responding to a stimulus (Henry & Rogers, 1960). The complexity of a movement is often considered to be related to the number of unique movement elements that must be coordinated. For example, an underhand toss is less complex than an overhand throw because the toss involves the movement of only the arm, forearm, and hand whereas the throw often requires a strict timing and sequencing involving the entire body. You will recall from chapter 5 that many actions are thought to be controlled through a motor program that sends signals from the central nervous system to make certain muscles contract in a specific pattern to produce a coordinated movement. Once we have selected a motor program during the response selection stage, we need to prepare to transmit the information in the program to our muscles. Some researchers think that the program must be constructed during the response programming stage. If more complex movements require more complex motor programs, it makes sense that the amount of time spent during response programming increases with movement complexity.

Reacting Faster: Ways to Reduce the Time Spent on Information Processing

So far, this discussion of information processing has focused mainly on the basic capabilities of humans and the limitations they impose on our performance. There are, however, additional considerations that allow us to use this information to enhance performance. With extensive amounts of practice, it does appear that both stimulus identification and response programming speed can be improved. Research shows that experts in some sports scan the field in a way that differs from the way their less experienced counterparts do (Williams & Davids, 1998). Some researchers have argued that experts learn to detect patterns in the environment and extract "chunks" of relevant information while novices tend to look at each aspect of the environment individually (Chase & Simon, 1973). For example, an expert soccer player might look at two locations on the field and immediately detect two distinct formations created by six defending players. In contrast, a novice might look at each player in turn; and even if he did eventually figure out the formations, it would likely be far too late to react in an effective manner. Response programming seems to benefit from practice as well. This is probably due to extensive practice in "assembling" motor programs in response to specific stimuli. The more we practice, the faster we get.

Both of these improvements (in stimulus identification and response programming) will probably yield only relatively small improvements in reaction time. Moreover, when unpredictability in the performance setting requires decision making, the response selection stage can take so long that any improvements in the other two stages might be barely noticeable. That is why open skills are said to emphasize decision-making demands. Even though they clearly place demands on the other two stages of information processing, the response selection stage seems to have the biggest impact on reaction time and performance.

TECHNOLOGY HIGHLIGHT

Eye Tracking

Eye-tracking equipment is used to measure where people are looking as they engage in a task. One way to accomplish this is to use two small cameras fitted onto eyeglasses or mounted to the head by other means. One camera records the scene that the person with the eye tracker is viewing, while the other camera is pointed at the person's eye. A computer program can use this information to calculate where the person is looking. The pictures show how this monitoring looks on a computer interface for an eye tracker. The picture on the left shows the view from the camera that is pointed at the eye, and the picture on the right shows the scene that the person was observing (the person was looking at and around the man standing on the balance board), with the actual pathway of focus superimposed on top of the object being viewed. In movement analysis, eye tracking can be used to determine where in the environment people find cues to guide their performance. For example, eye-tracking studies have been used to determine that expert and novice tennis players differ in terms of what they look at when preparing to receive an opponent's serve. Eye trackers can also tell us how long people look at a particular spot, which is called fixation time. Research has shown that experts in several different sports typically have longer fixation times than novices but that they focus on fewer locations in their environment (Vickers, 2007).

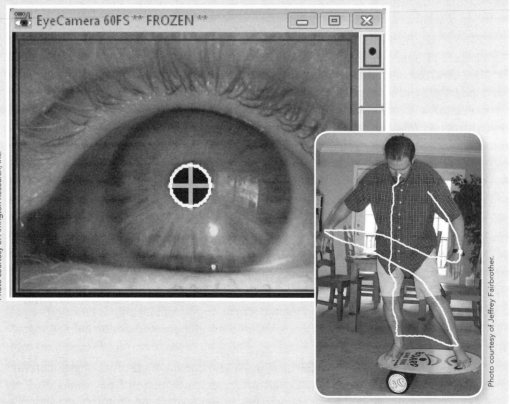

Photo courtesy of Arrington Research, Inc.

Photo courtesy of Jeffrey Fairbrother.

anticipation—Prediction of an upcoming stimulus in order to decide on a response in advance; anticipation of a foreseeable stimulus can dramatically reduce response time in that it eliminates decision making during the reaction.

So, how can we handle this limitation? Luckily, we are already very good at getting around this particular information processing demand by using **anticipation.** Remember that reaction time is defined as the amount of time to begin a response to an unexpected or *unanticipated* signal. In reality, we are actually fairly good at anticipating what will happen next and when it will happen because we are "tipped off" by information in the environment. For example, we know that a person standing on the side of the road may start to cross the street as we approach in our car, so we are ready to respond if we see something to cue us that this is indeed happening. In fact, the situations in which we cannot anticipate are much less frequent and usually result from some effort to control the environment to prevent anticipation. For instance, the starting procedures used in swimming and running races reduce the ability to anticipate. Our ability to effectively anticipate often allows us to decide on the appropriate response before we even detect the stimulus. In other words, we complete the response selection stage in advance, and so our reaction time is greatly reduced.

To effectively anticipate, we need to successfully predict a stimulus and know how to respond to it. We need to learn what the relevant cues are in the environment, when and where they occur, what the appropriate responses are, and how to execute them correctly. The use of anticipation to complete response selection is based on our accumulated body of knowledge regarding a specific performance situation. Tony Gwynn, a former professional baseball player, was famous for studying the habits of opposing pitchers so that he could learn their "tells" (i.e., the physical signs they inadvertently sent before a particular pitch), as well as calculate the probability of a given type of pitch in a given situation (e.g., he might know that a certain pitcher never threw a slider when the batter had more balls than strikes). Although this knowledge base is critically important in rapidly responding and making the correct decision, the performer also needs to know how to execute the responses in order to be successful.

Thus, efforts to improve information processing speed should focus on all three stages:

1. *Stimulus identification:* Performers should practice detecting information within the performance setting. This will strengthen their capabilities to detect patterns of information (e.g., a particular grouping of rugby players can indicate a certain play). It will also help them to learn about the regular features of the setting so they can know where to focus during performance. For example, to detect the movement of opponents, players in sports such as hockey and soccer are often told to watch the midsection and ignore the limbs.

2. *Response selection:* Performers should learn to bypass this stage (actually complete it in advance) by using correct anticipation. They can do this by learning about the characteristics of opponents and performance settings so they know what to expect.

3. *Response programming:* Performers should practice responding to the actual task demands of the performance. This will shorten the time it takes to prepare their responses when transferring to the performance setting. It will also ensure that that their movements are executed effectively.

Of course, anticipation also has two obvious drawbacks. The first and most problematic is the cost associated with making the wrong decision (Schmidt & Wrisberg, 2008). Obviously, if we select the wrong response, then the advantage we gain by reacting quickly is lost. Take, for example, the case of a cornerback in American football whose job is to cover wide receivers and prevent a pass reception (or make an interception). If a cornerback incorrectly anticipates that the quarterback will throw the ball to a certain location and then moves to that location, he may be too far out of position to defend against the actual throw. Consequently, the receiver he was covering will have an easier job catching the ball and moving it downfield toward the end zone. In this case, the goals of the cornerback's team would have been better served had he not anticipated. Don't take this example as an argument against anticipation, though. It would be impossible to be an effective cornerback without anticipating.

The fact that we anticipate so frequently in our daily lives suggests that in most cases, the benefits of anticipating outweigh the costs. We just need to make sure we practice our anticipation skills for those tasks that rely heavily on them. If we are not particularly good at anticipation in a certain skill setting, it may be better to react slowly than to make an outright mistake. For example, if you play on a recreational soccer team and you have trouble reading the intentions of some of your opponents as they dribble the ball, it is probably not a good idea to make a move based on your best guess only to have the other player dribble easily past you. Instead, your best move might be to stay in front of the ball to slow the play down enough to allow your teammates to help out. Putting some distance between you and the other player may not be a great way to play defense, but it will allow you a bit more time to react so that you can at least stay between your goal and the ball.

The second drawback to anticipation is seen when the person focuses more on the decision than the action. It seems that people's capabilities in anticipating and in executing responses both limit how well they might perform. Although it is important to improve anticipation skills, it is unlikely that these skills will push a person to higher levels of performance if she lacks the physical proficiency to execute the appropriate responses. For example, we have learned from interviews of tennis players of varying competitive levels that the knowledge required for tactical decision making (e.g., anticipation) increases as performance skill increases (McPherson, 1999; McPherson & Kernodle, 2007). This suggests that tennis players do not learn to anticipate beyond their physical skill level. Thus, if people place too much emphasis on developing anticipation skills, especially to the extent that this effort takes away from the development of physical skills, their overall performance will probably not improve. A better approach is to ensure that their practice incorporates both learning to anticipate and working on physical skills.

How We Pay Attention

In the previous discussion of anticipation, it was probably fairly clear that one of the things you need to learn to anticipate effectively is what information to pay attention to. We all know from experience that we have a limited **attentional capacity.** That is, we cannot pay attention to everything. Instead, we must selectively direct our attention to the information that we feel will serve our purposes (Prezuhy & Etnier, 2001). This phenomenon has some important implications for the performance of

> **attentional capacity**—The amount of information that we can attend to at any given time; limitations in our attentional capacity force us to selectively devote attention to those aspects of our movements that we think are the most relevant.

motor skills, whether we are hammering a nail or blocking in volleyball. Our limited capacity to pay attention can degrade our performances when there is a large amount of information available that must be used to guide our performance. This limitation can be clearly seen in new learners, who often struggle to complete a task in its entirety.

Imagine, for example, that I want to teach you how to tie a bowline knot (assuming you do not already know). I will probably demonstrate the steps accompanied by a verbal "walk-through" to show you the whole skill. After I finish my instructions, there is a good chance that you will remember either the first step or the last step, but that you will forget at least one of the important intermediate steps. This is because you do not have enough attentional capacity to be able to keep all of the previous steps in your working memory while you are following my explanation of the current step. With some experience, however, you will commit the steps to memory so that you will be able to complete the entire knot-tying task on your own. Because the task is still relatively new to you, this will require quite a bit of attentional effort. Your performance will be slow, and it is unlikely that you will be able to do anything else while tying the knot. If you keep practicing, you will ultimately get to the point where you have to devote very little attention to tying the knot, and you will be able to use "spare" attentional capacity to do other things at the same time (e.g., walking or talking).

The fact that we can direct our attention serves a useful function to help us deal with our limited attentional capacity. We can choose to pay attention to some information and ignore other information. In the knot-tying example, a motivated learner will direct her full attention to the instructions and attempt to ignore other information (e.g., noise in the room or hunger pangs). If she cannot remember all of the steps after the initial instruction, there is a chance that she will choose to direct her attention to the beginning steps during subsequent instructions. For example, she might focus on the first step, and then on the first two steps, and then on the first three steps, and so on until she is able to remember all of the steps. If she were not able to direct her attention selectively, she would never be able to gradually learn skills that entail too much information for early learners to grasp all at once.

As her knot tying begins to improve, the learner may direct her attention to aspects of her performance other than the basic steps. For example, she may focus on the way she moves her hands, looking for more effective strategies. In tying a bowline knot, there are a number of shortcuts that people typically discover as they continue to practice if they devote some of their attention to looking for more effective ways to tie the knot. Once her knot tying becomes fairly automatic, she will probably begin to devote some of her attention to other things as she ties the knot. Emergency responders sometimes use the bowline to tie a loop around someone who is stranded, for example on a cliff or on a rock in a river. In such a situation, it is beneficial that the rescuer does not need to devote much attention to tying the knot and can instead focus mostly on assessing the victim and the rescue situation.

What We Pay Attention to Makes a Difference

Another benefit of being able to direct our attention is the fact that we can (for the most part) decide what we pay attention to. This aspect of how we pay attention is often referred to as **attentional focus.** Where we direct our attention can influence

> **attentional focus**—A characteristic of our capability to selectively direct attention to specific sources of information; the object of our focus.

our performance. In terms of information processing, we of course always want to focus on information relevant to the task, but the source of the "best" information is not always clear. Attentional focus can be broken into two dimensions (Nideffer, 1976). The first of these has to do with how narrowly or broadly we focus our attention. At times, a broad focus is appropriate when we need to gather a great deal of information, for example when we play a team sport that requires us to monitor several opponents. In other instances, a narrower focus might be better. For example, a weightlifter performing a squat might focus his attention on keeping his back straight. The second dimension of attentional focus concerns whether our focus is directed internally or externally. We adopt an internal focus when we monitor sensations in our body or concentrate on our thoughts. We adopt an external focus when we direct our attention toward events and objects outside of our own body. These two dimensions can be combined to create four categories of attentional focus: narrow-internal, broad-internal, narrow-external, and broad-external.

Several examples can be identified for each of the four categories of attentional focus. A narrow-internal focus involves directing attention to relatively few sources of information within the body. A person rehabilitating an injured knee might focus on achieving increased knee extension when she walks. A hockey goalie might focus on a mental cue to keep the knees closed during practice to improve his defensive posture. A broad-internal focus involves directing attention either to a general feeling or to several sources of information within the body. A surfer might focus on the general feeling of jumping to her feet as she catches a wave. A runner might focus on a feeling of general fatigue (i.e., "low energy") as he nears the end of a race. A narrow-external focus involves directing attention to relatively few sources of information in the environment. A baseball pitcher might focus on the catcher's mitt if no runners are on base. A rock climber might focus on a handhold as she reaches for it. A broad-external focus involves directing attention to several sources of information in the environment. A forward in soccer might monitor the movements of three defenders in different locations on the field as she plans an attack. A driver might focus on several cars, street signs, and pedestrians as he navigates a busy city intersection.

Skill Insight

Focusing your attention on something in the environment has been shown to enhance motor performance and learning. Gaby Wulf and her colleagues have examined the effects of asking learners to adopt either an internal or external focus of attention while practicing actions such as a volleyball serve or a soccer pass (Wulf et al., 2002). For an internal focus, learners typically direct their attention toward controlling parts of their body used in the task (e.g., using your instep to contact the ball when kicking). An external focus usually directs attention toward objects or locations in the environment (e.g., moving the ball toward the target). It has been suggested that performance suffers for some actions when a person tries to consciously control his or her movements. In golf, this phenomenon has sometimes been referred to as "paralysis through analysis" (i.e., overthinking the swing).

Any decision about where to direct your attention should be guided by an understanding of how this focus might be expected to enhance your performance. Adopting a given focus might be beneficial or detrimental depending upon the task, the person, or the particular focus. For example, some highly experienced distance runners might adopt a narrow-internal focus on their pattern of breathing to help them regulate their running pace (Silva & Applebaum, 1989). In contrast, an inexperienced runner who adopts an internal-narrow focus on a pain in her foot may find that her performance suffers.

Recent research indicates that for some tasks, adopting an external focus will benefit performance compared to adopting an internal focus (Wulf, 2007a). Traditional instruction in movement settings such as sport has relied heavily on directing performers' attention to their own pattern of movement involved in an action (e.g., how the player should position his feet as he passes the soccer ball, or what arm movements should be used in making a basketball free throw). This recent line of research suggests that it is often better to focus our attention on the effects of the movements (e.g., the player receiving the pass or the basketball goal) rather than the movements themselves. These demonstrations that an external focus can sometimes be superior to an internal focus should remind us that progress is sometimes made through questioning conventional wisdom. On the other hand, we are not yet to the point where we can say that an external focus is always best. The recommended approach is to develop instructions that direct the learner's attention to relevant cues while not overloading attentional capacity.

Arousal and Performance

As we consider the role of attention in the performance of motor skills, it is important that we also recognize how a person's arousal can influence performance (Wrisberg, 1994). You can think of arousal as reflecting your level of mental and physical energy. At very low levels of arousal, you are not devoting much mental or physical energy toward completing whatever task you are doing. Think about a teenager who is asked to take out the garbage. Most of the time, he will do it only because his parents make him; he won't be very interested in the task. He will devote as little attention (mental energy) and physical effort (physical energy) as he can to the job while still getting it done. Maybe he will drag the bag along the floor as he slowly shuffles toward the garbage can, reading his text messages along the way. Fortunately, the standard for successful garbage transfer is not too high, and the teenager will likely get the job done despite his low arousal level. However, it is also easy to imagine that he could complete the job faster if he devoted even a moderate amount of attention to it.

As your arousal level increases from its lowest levels, so does your performance of any given motor skill (Yerkes & Dodson, 1908). Initial improvements in your performance probably reflect the fact that you decided to direct your attention toward the goals of the task. After that point, further increases in arousal help you to focus your attention squarely on the task and devote the appropriate physical effort to completing the required movements. At some point, usually at moderate levels of arousal, you will reach the peak of your performance. This is when you will be operating most effectively in terms of achieving the goals of the task in which you are engaged. Further increases in arousal will actually begin to degrade your performance as you become overaroused for the task.

Arousal affects your performance because it influences your capability to pay attention. At low levels of arousal, your attention will be very broad and you will focus on many cues that are not relevant to the task you are doing. A great example of this is the young child playing outfield in baseball who is paying attention to everything but the game. As arousal increases, however, the scope of your attention starts to narrow (Weltman & Egstrom, 1966). During this narrowing of attention, you start to disregard information that is not important to your performance until you reach a point at which you are paying attention to all of the relevant cues but not to anything else. This is typified by the athlete who is "in the zone." If your arousal increases even further, your attention will continue to narrow until you start actually missing some of those relevant cues that you noticed earlier. Imagine that our baseball player is a pitcher rather than an outfielder. Overarousal can hurt a pitcher's performance when he becomes so focused on striking out a batter that he forgets to check the runner on first base. Other examples can be seen in a wide variety of performance settings. For example, a gymnast might be so focused on completing a particular stunt that she does not notice that she will land out of bounds. A surgeon might be so focused on suturing an incision that she fails to monitor the patient's vital signs. Eventually, extremely high levels of arousal can cause attention to become so narrowly focused that you cannot even perform the task anymore (because you miss so much necessary information).

One way to ensure that people perform at their best is to help them reach their optimal range of arousal. This range has been called the **individual zone of optimal functioning** (IZOF; Hanin, 2000). As the name implies, one person's IZOF may be different from another's. For example, I might function well at a slightly higher level of arousal when putting a golf

individual zone of optimal functioning (IZOF)—The range of arousal within which an individual's performance is at its peak.

ball compared to you. Both of us, however, will probably function best when we are in the middle of the range of arousal across which each of us can actually putt. The location of the IZOF with respect to the level of arousal can also be influenced by the specific demands of the task you are completing (Schmidt & Wrisberg, 2008; Weinberg & Hunt, 1976). Tasks that require a great deal of thinking and fine motor coordination are typically performed at relatively low levels of arousal (compared to the arousal required for other tasks). Examples might include an artist completing fine details on a painting or a dentist carefully working to drill out a cavity. Tasks that are mostly physical and involve whole body coordination require higher levels of arousal. Examples of these types of tasks include playing offensive line in American football or competing in a keg toss event in the World's Strongest Man competition. Many of the motor skills we perform will fall somewhere between these two extremes, requiring a moderate level of arousal.

Speed–Accuracy Trade-Offs

You have probably experienced speed–accuracy trade-offs many times as you have completed various tasks (Fitts, 1954). For example, you know from experience that the faster you move your computer mouse, the more likely you are to miss the icon you are moving to click. Similarly, you also know that you need to slow down to ensure that your key goes into the lock when you want to open your front door. Both of these examples demonstrate the fact that many tasks require us to trade between speed and accuracy in our movements. This is usually not a problem until we are faced with a task that gives us a limited amount of time to respond. When we are compelled to act quickly, we can sometimes emphasize speed over accuracy and actually end up missing the goal of the task entirely. For example, think about how many times you have hurriedly reached to flip a light switch as you passed by it without slowing your stride. Because you knew that you had one short opportunity to hit the switch, you probably emphasized speed and in some cases missed the switch completely. What I find interesting about this particular situation is how our perceived need to act fast often initiates a cycle of several reaches and misses, which ends up taking far longer than if we had simply slowed down in the first place.

Sometimes, however, we might favor accuracy over speed. This might happen when we are just getting the hang of a skill. Because we cannot complete the skill quickly, we tend to focus on just getting it done. This can be problematic if there is a limited amount of time to complete the task. For example, a beginning music student might methodically work his way through all the notes of a song only to realize that his slow pace did not result in a recognizable tune. I've used a speed–accuracy trade-off activity in my classes for many years and have seen some interesting behaviors. In my experience, certain people have a very difficult time trying to balance the speed and accuracy demands in a task that requires them to tap back and forth between two targets. Some people cannot seem to slow down even though they continually miss the target, while other people move so slowly that it stretches the imagination to use the word "speed" in connection with the task they are supposed to be completing.

Skill Insight

Sometimes moving faster can make you more accurate. Although the general rule is that we trade speed for accuracy (or vice versa) when we make aiming movements, there are a couple of exceptions. Dick Schmidt and his colleagues have shown that when we move very rapidly to begin with, speeding up can make us more consistent in timing a movement (Schmidt et al., 1979) and in where we end the movement compared to our target (Schmidt & Sherwood, 1982). This research suggests that faster might be better if the action requires us to move rapidly in the first place. For example, you need to swing an axe quite forcefully if you want to chop wood, so working to improve the speed of your swings might increase the accuracy of your blade placement on the tree or log. This does not mean, however, that you should go out and swing as hard as you can. Such a strategy would likely result in sloppy and very dangerous performance. Instead, it means that you might improve your accuracy if you work to gradually increase the speed of well-controlled swings.

Many tasks have both speed and accuracy requirements. Often the best way to approach these tasks is to try to move as fast as you can without sacrificing accuracy. This might apply to taking a shot on goal in a hockey game or swinging a cricket bat. Both of these examples illustrate tasks that must be completed quickly but that depend on a high degree of accuracy. After all, it does not matter how quickly you can kick a soccer ball if you always miss the goal. If, on the other hand, you are usually very accurate when you complete these types of tasks, you might try speeding up a bit to gain a greater advantage. If you miss your target too often, then you should slow down.

Abilities and Skills

I will end this chapter by discussing the distinction between motor abilities and **motor skills.** Although we often use these terms interchangeably, they actually refer to distinct concepts (Schmidt & Wrisberg, 2008). **Motor abilities** are those movement capabilities that we possess because of our genetic makeup. In other words, we are born with them. This does not mean, however, that we are able to use all of our abilities at birth. Most motor abilities develop over time as a person matures to adulthood. The important thing to remember is that abilities are not learned. Everybody possesses them to varying degrees. For example, the ability to react quickly to an unexpected stimulus is something all healthy people possess. Remember that reaction time is the span of time from when an *unexpected* cue is presented until the beginning of

motor ability—A biologically determined capability to produce a specific type of movement response.

motor skill—A learned or experience-based capability to produce a movement response.

a response. Some of us may be faster than others (reflecting the strength of each of our individual abilities to process information), but it is unlikely that any one of us can improve our reaction time no matter how much we practice (showing that this is not a learned response).

In contrast to a motor ability, a motor skill is a capability to move that we acquire through experience or practice. In other words, we *learn* motor skills. The vast majority of complex real-world movement activities, such as brushing your teeth, using a screwdriver, or making a layup in basketball, are skills; so it is important to recognize that both innate abilities and learned characteristics contribute to your performance when you complete them.

Abilities typically refer to our capabilities to complete fairly specific movement responses. For example, we might think about a person's abilities to move his fingers precisely (finger dexterity), match the movements of his hands and feet (multilimb coordination), or hold his hand steady (arm-hand steadiness) (Fleishman, 1964). Skills, on the other hand, involve more complex demands and often rely on a combination of abilities as well as acquired knowledge. For example, tying a knot relies on finger dexterity and coordination of multiple limbs (usually two hands), but also knowledge of the steps involved in tying the knot. You might have been born with a great deal of finger dexterity and multilimb coordination, but you had to *learn* the skill of knot tying.

It is fairly common for people to attribute success in movement activities such as sports to motor abilities, or natural gifts. Although abilities play a role, it is a mistake to think that they are the reason for a person's success. Researchers who study expert performance in movement skills have noted that practice is the single most important factor contributing to achieving expertise (Ericsson, Krampe, & Tesch-Römer, 1993). For the vast majority of us, we have reached our current level of proficiency in whatever sport (or other movement activity) we engage in not because of our genetic makeup, but because of the amount of high-quality practice we have completed. It does, however, make sense that abilities might be important in distinguishing between any two highly skilled performers because they have probably accumulated a similar amount of practice. So, abilities might be the determining factor that distinguishes between two professional golfers such as Tiger Woods and Phil Mickelson, but the amount of practice (and the skill that results) is what accounts for the difference between an average recreational golfer and an average club professional.

 To become an able man in any profession, there are three things necessary, nature, study, and practice.

Henry Ward Beecher

Recognizing the role of abilities is important for at least two reasons. First, it reminds us that individual differences between learners can affect how well a person performs at any given point during the learning process. Thus, instructors should attempt to tailor their approaches to individual needs and preferences when this is possible and appropriate. However, an instructor should never attempt to identify a learner's abilities (genetic makeup) with the goal of determining this person's ultimate potential for a sport or motor skill. Although abilities certainly play a role in the individual differences that we observe at any given time, a person's prior experience and training also contribute to how well he can perform the skill.

If instructors overemphasize abilities, they may mistakenly assume that a person's future performance can be predicted by how well the person currently performs. The first problem with this idea is that we know that people's proficiency will change as they practice and develop more skill. The second problem is that the abilities that contribute to success in a movement activity may change quite dramatically as a person progresses from one level of performance to another. For example, being a fast runner is a tremendous advantage in youth soccer. High scorers often just kick the ball downfield and then beat everyone else to it. When we consider professional soccer, however, we see that running speed is not a very useful way to distinguish between players; almost all of them are fast. The third problem is that many outside factors may influence a person's development regardless of her innate abilities. For example, a lack of support from family and friends, limited access to facilities (or equipment or coaches), or an injury can all act to prevent a person from achieving a desired goal.

The second, and more important, reason for focusing on skills instead of abilities relates to the fact that we can teach people skills but have no control over their abilities. A skill focus emphasizes helping everyone to maximize each person's training by using our understanding of the principles of motor behavior. Because most of us will never attain extremely high levels of performance in most of our movement skills (we're not likely to be going to the National Basketball Association or to become a master carpenter), it makes the most sense to adopt an inclusive approach that encourages learners to improve their performance no matter what their initial level of proficiency.

The Short of It

- We process information from the environment to help us to prepare and control our movements. This processing occurs in at least three stages, which involve the identification of information (stimulus identification), decision making (response selection), and preparation of the body (motor programming).
- By learning to predict regular features in performance settings, we can use anticipation to dramatically improve the speed of our responses.
- Although we have a limited attentional capacity, we can direct our attentional focus to the sources of information that are most relevant for the performance of our movements.
- As our level of arousal increases, our attentional focus will narrow. At first, this helps us focus only on the information that is important for our task. If we get overaroused, however, our attention will become so narrow that we will miss relevant cues and our performance will suffer.

- Our performance in tasks that require both speed and accuracy can sometimes be compromised by a tendency to favor one over the other. Emphasizing speed often results in reduced accuracy, and emphasizing accuracy often results in responding too late to be effective. When we are performing such tasks, it is sometimes helpful to think about performing as fast as we can without sacrificing accuracy.

- Training should adopt a skill focus to help each person maximize his or her individual level of performance.

CHAPTER 7

Setting Practice Procedures

In this chapter you will learn the following:

✓ How varied practice can be used to help learners develop flexibility in the way they execute a skill

✓ How blocked and random practice schedules affect immediate performance during practice and long-term learning

✓ How the amount of time that is allowed to pass between trials of a task or between practice sessions can influence learning

✓ Some practical considerations to help an instructor choose an appropriate practice schedule for a given learner, task, and performance setting

To understand the human form means to understand the body in motion.

Fritjof Capra (2007)

One of the challenges faced by physical therapists is determining the most effective way to implement a variety of therapy activities to help patients recover as much function as possible. For example, a physical therapist working with a stroke patient may want to emphasize three different aspects of movement with a debilitated arm: reaching for and grasping an object, transporting an object, and manipulating an object. Should the therapist schedule practice on each of these tasks separately so that the patient can devote his or her full effort to learning one thing at a time? Or perhaps it would be better to schedule practice on all three tasks during each practice session. If the therapist does decide to include all three tasks, it will be necessary to determine the order in which to present the tasks. These scheduling decisions may seem somewhat trivial, but research suggests otherwise. There are, in fact, specific considerations that can help the therapist determine which schedule is most appropriate for the patient's rehabilitation goals.

■   ■   ■

So far in this book, you have read mostly about the different types of demands that various motor skills involve and the capabilities and limitations of humans in meeting these demands. In many of the examples, I have also discussed some of the ways in which a given performance setting might be expected to influence these task demands and learner characteristics. For example, when performing a musical piece during a recital, a normally anxious piano player will be more likely to become overaroused compared to one who is typically calm. The reason is that the presence of an audience in this particular performance setting interacts with the piano player's anxiety. The high level of arousal that results may interfere with the performance of fine motor skills required in playing a piano. In contrast, the calmer performance setting that exists during regular practice may not bother the anxious piano player much, so we might not be able to detect any differences between the two players until the recital.

> *I am always doing that which I cannot do, in order that I may learn how to do it.*
>
> **Pablo Picasso**

Another example of these types of interactions can be seen when we try to transfer our motor skills from practice to the real world. It is fairly common for novice tennis players to hit forehand ground strokes over and over during practice. This type of practice does not reflect the true demands of hitting such a shot in a game, however, because it does not require the player to learn other important skills. In a game, almost every shot is preceded by a fairly unique set of circumstances related to the player's previous stroke (e.g., backhand, volley, smash, or forehand) and location on the court, as well as the type of shot just made by the opponent and where it is headed relative to the player's current position. As a player begins to master the basic tennis strokes, the coach might want to organize practice drills that introduce some of these demands. As this tennis example shows, it is important to know about the different ways a practice setting might be structured when attempting to help someone learn a new movement skill or refine an existing one. In addition, professionals should understand how these different practice structures affect performance not only during the practice session but also under circumstances that will call for reliance on long-term learning. In this chapter, I will introduce you to three concepts related to the number of tasks practiced during a session (constant and varied practice), the order in which tasks are presented if more than one is practiced (blocked and random practice), and the amount of rest allowed between practice attempts (practice distribution).

Constant and Varied Practice

One of the basic choices you will face when you begin to design an instructional experience is whether to ask the learner to practice more than one task during a session. Your decision will depend upon the nature of the task as well as the setting in which the learner will eventually perform. Figure 7.1 illustrates the differences between constant and varied practice. **Constant practice** refers to a situation in which the learner practices a single task during an entire practice session. A good example of this is seen when a basketball player goes to the gym to shoot only free throws. One of the benefits of constant practice is that it allows the learner to complete a relatively large number of trials (practice attempts) on a single skill. This is probably appropriate when the skill is always performed in situations that closely match the practice session (e.g., Giuffrida, Shea, & Fairbrother, 2002; Keetch et al., 2005). A free throw is always attempted with a standard ball, aimed at a standard goal, from a set distance. One of the drawbacks of constant practice is that it generally prevents the learner from developing flexibility in his or her responses.

constant practice—A type of practice schedule in which the learner practices only one task variation during an entire practice session.

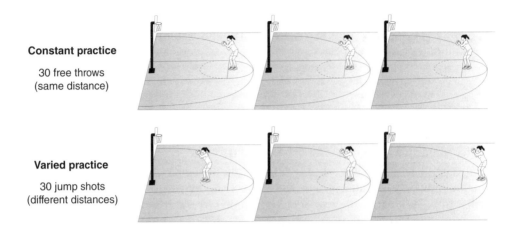

Constant practice

30 free throws
(same distance)

Varied practice

30 jump shots
(different distances)

FIGURE 7.1   Constant practice involving repetition of a single task variation versus varied practice involving three different task variations.

Another example of constant practice that illustrates both its potential benefits and drawbacks can be seen when an occupational therapist asks a patient to move an object (e.g., a can of food) from a counter to a shelf several times in a row. In this case, the therapist might choose constant practice because the patient needs to develop a foundation of strength to simply complete the activity. In other words, the goal at this point involves simply completing the basic task components of lifting, reaching, and setting. Because this single exercise is not a very good representation of the demands that the patient will eventually face in daily life, however, the therapist will at some point probably move away from using constant practice. Eventually, the patient will need to learn how to perform the task in different ways (e.g., by lifting cans of varying weights). In the next section, I will describe *varied practice,* which is a common way of using task variations to help learners develop flexibility in their capabilities to produce movements.

In chapter 5, I described how movements are thought to be controlled by generalized motor programs. These motor programs maintain the overall pattern of a movement but can be scaled to meet different demands (e.g., completing the entire task faster or slower, or with more or less force). I used the example of a dart throw to demonstrate how changing the force of the throw would cause a dart to travel a given distance in different amounts of time. This is important because a relatively slow-moving dart will drop down quite a bit as it travels to the board. For throwing any object, we all know from experience that a more forceful throw will make the object travel farther or cover a given distance in less time (i.e., it will move faster). The generalized motor program is a means of storing in memory our understanding of rules like the one that relates force to distance for throwing.

When a skill calls for flexibility in aspects related to how forceful or fast the entire movement should be, **varied practice** is likely to be more helpful than constant practice (Schmidt & Wrisberg, 2008). This is also true for movements that are scaled in terms of the entire distance covered during the movement. For example, most dance steps can be completed using short, medium, or long steps as long as the overall pattern of the movement is fixed. This idea of scaling is also illustrated in the earlier example of the occupational therapist who asks a patient to place different-sized cans on a shelf. The overall pattern of movement for lifting most cans is the same (e.g., the sequence of movements and their relationship to one another), but moving a heavier can will require more force during each stage. In this case, varied practice helps the patient develop the flexibility to apply the appropriate force when lifting cans of different weights.

varied practice—A practice schedule in which the learner practices more than one variation of a task. The typical means of creating these variations is to scale a fixed movement pattern in terms of its overall distance, speed, or force.

In varied practice, the learner practices more than one variation of a given skill. Remember that from the perspective of schema theory, the generalized motor program is what contains the information needed to perform any given motor skill (Schmidt, 1975). Varied practice is thought to work by allowing the learner to practice setting parameters (e.g., more or less force) and get a better feel for the "rule" (or schema) that links the result of the movement to the parameter value that was set. In other words, we learn that lifting heavier cans requires more force than lifting lighter cans. This may seem obvious, but if you have ever picked up a nearly empty milk carton that you thought was full, you have experienced what happens when you set your force parameter incorrectly. Because the goal is to develop flexibility in our use of a given generalized motor program, varied practice uses skill variations that are all in the same class of movements (i.e., they are all governed by a single generalized motor program). So, task variations differ mostly in terms of the force or time needed to accomplish the entire movement. A jump shot in basketball is a great example. Basketball players need to take jump shots from a wide variety of distances, so they need to learn the relationship between the distance to the basket and how hard to shoot the ball. Shooting from a variety of distances will strengthen their generalized motor program for the jump shot and increase the likelihood that they will select the appropriate amount of force even when they shoot from a totally new distance.

The idea that varied practice can strengthen a generalized motor program would not apply to situations in which several unrelated skills

Skill Insight

Recovering stroke patients can learn motor skills more effectively by practicing more than one task at a time. Robert Hanlon asked patients recovering from a stroke to practice a task that required them to simulate the movements needed to retrieve a coffee cup from a cupboard (Hanlon, 1996). These movements included opening the cupboard door, grasping the handle of the cup, lifting the cup out of the cupboard, setting the cup down, and then releasing the cup. One group practiced just the cup-retrieval task while another group also practiced three related tasks that involved pointing, touching objects, or touching spots on a surface. The results indicated that the patients who practiced more than one task learned the cup-retrieval task better than the group that practiced just one task. This study suggests that practicing a set of related movement tasks can help stroke patients recover certain functions better than when they focus on only one activity at a time.

> *Once a conceptual understanding of the [physical therapy] program is actualized, the patient is able to see the relationship between a specific exercise and the related functional skill.*

Jan Harrington (1984)

(in terms of the overall movement pattern) are practiced together. For example, practicing free throws, layups, and dunks during the same practice session should not strengthen the generalized motor program of any of these skills because there is little opportunity for the learner to practice setting different parameter values for any one of the skills. There are, however, other reasons why practicing unrelated skills together might benefit learning. In the next section, I will discuss blocked and random practice schedules to illustrate how the order in which a learner practices multiple skills can influence learning.

Skill Insight

Allowing a learner to control some aspect of an instructional setting can benefit learning (Wulf, 2007b). Several studies have addressed this so-called self-control effect using a variety of tasks. These studies have examined skiing using a ski simulator, a badminton long serve, a basketball free throw, table tennis, and tossing a ball or beanbag. Learners have been allowed to control how often they receive feedback, watch a demonstration video, or use physical assistance devices (i.e., ski poles on the ski simulator). In almost every case, participants who were given some self control learned the skills better than participants who were not given any control. It is still unknown why self-control works to enhance learning, but some researchers have argued that it may increase the learners' motivation or give them the opportunity to engage more deeply with the task. Interestingly, participants in self-control conditions typically reduce their requests for instructional support as they move through practice. So, at some level, it seems that learners have an understanding of when they need help and recognize that they should learn to perform skills independently.

Blocked and Random Practice

Blocked and random practice schedules represent two different ways of presenting practice trials when more than one skill is being learned during a single practice session (figure 7.2). In a **blocked practice** schedule, the learner practices one task at a time before moving on to another task. For example, a cricket practice might incorporate three different stations. At the first station, the player would practice 25 trials of a fielding drill in a position close to the batsman (close fielding); he would then move to the second station to practice 25 trials of a fielding drill in a position farther away from the batsman (intermediate fielding). Finally, he would move to the third station to practice 25 trials of throwing toward the stumps (i.e., the wickets behind the batsman). In a blocked schedule such as this, all of the trials on one skill are completed before practice

blocked practice—A practice schedule in which the learner completes all trials of one task before moving on to practice the next task.

random practice—A practice schedule in which the learner completes trials of various tasks presented in a random order.

is begun on another skill. In a **random practice** schedule, trials of the skills to be practiced are presented in what is essentially a random order. For example, the coach could implement the cricket practice by developing a schedule in advance such that each player rotates through the three stations (e.g., close fielding, throwing at the stumps, intermediate fielding) in a fairly unpredictable order. Random practice has been shown to enhance learning for a wide variety of motor skills despite the fact that it often degrades immediate performance during the practice session itself. In contrast, blocked practice often results in impressive performance during practice, but less long-term learning (Fairbrother, Hall, & Shea, 2002; Fairbrother, Shea, & Marzilli, 2007; Shea & Morgan, 1979).

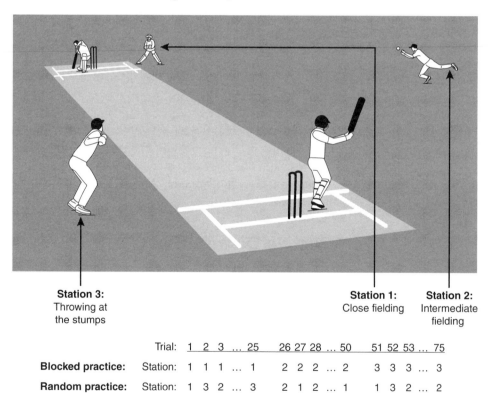

		Trial:	1	2	3	…	25	26	27	28	…	50	51	52	53	…	75
Blocked practice:	Station:		1	1	1	…	1	2	2	2	…	2	3	3	3	…	3
Random practice:	Station:		1	3	2	…	3	2	1	2	…	1	1	3	2	…	2

FIGURE 7.2 An example of blocked and random practice schedules in cricket. In the blocked schedule, the athletes practice close fielding, then intermediate fielding, then throwing at stumps. In the random schedule, the athletes move from drill to drill in a random order.

Both blocked and random practice schedules have their place during motor skill instruction. It is thought that one of the reasons random practice enhances learning is that it introduces an appropriate challenge to the learner (Guadagnoli & Lee, 2004). That is, switching from one task to another is harder than simply repeating the same task. Some researchers have suggested that this experience is analogous to what happens when a person is asked to solve simple math problems (Lee & Magill, 1983). If I ask you to answer the question, "What is 51 + 17?", you will do a little mental arithmetic and tell me "68." If I ask you the same question again, you will simply tell me the answer without working through the process to get the solution. You already have the solution, and you will just remember it. In this example, repeating the question will not improve your addition skills. Blocked practice of fairly simple motor skills may promote the same type of behavior. The learner simply remembers the response but does not really practice "solving the movement problem."

In a random practice schedule, however, switching to a new task is thought to cause the learner to forget some of the solution to the previous task (Lee & Magill, 1985). Imagine a basketball player in a random practice schedule that moves her from a chest pass to a layup. The idea here is that when she switches to the layup, she will forget some of the aspects of completing an effective chest pass. When she tries to complete another chest pass, she has to solve the problem again. As a result, she needs to put more effort into completing the chest pass (compared to just doing it over and over), and this effort promotes long-term learning. Other researchers believe that random practice allows the learner to make comparisons between the skills they are practicing (Shea & Zimny, 1983, 1988). For example, a learner in our basketball practice might note that the flight of the ball is affected by wrist flexion in both the chest pass and the layup. Random practice is also thought to promote comparisons between existing knowledge and the skills currently being practiced. For example, the learner might note that dribbling a basketball shares some similarity with dribbling a soccer ball because both tasks require the performer to control the ball while looking ahead (instead of at the ball). It is also reasonable to think that random practice might simply be more motivating because it introduces a more game-like atmosphere than does blocked practice.

Practice Distribution

Practice distribution refers to the amount of time that passes between successive attempts at a skill or between practice sessions. Within a single practice session, a **massed practice** schedule gives the learner brief rests between trials. Typically, the rest time is no longer than the amount of time it takes to complete a task. Imagine that a person practicing rifle shooting takes 5 to 7 seconds to sight the target and squeeze the trigger. A massed practice schedule would require the shooter to begin sighting the next target before 5 seconds have passed since the previous shot. Massed practice can also refer to situations in which practice sessions are closely spaced. For example, a restaurant might

massed practice—A practice schedule in which very little time passes between successive trials, usually no longer than the time required to complete the task. Massed practice also refers to situations in which practice is scheduled into relatively few sessions.

TECHNOLOGY HIGHLIGHT

Computerized Testing

One of the ways in which issues of practice scheduling have been examined is through research using computer software that can record the amount of time it takes a participant to respond to a stimulus (that is, reaction time) by pressing a key on a keyboard, as well as the time to move from one key to another. In several studies, participants have been asked to learn three different key-pressing sequences. The images below show a screen shot from a program called E-Prime that I have used in some of my research and a diagram used to indicate the sequence of keys to be pressed on the computer's keypad. By using computer-controlled procedures, researchers can easily manipulate the order in which tasks are presented while also ensuring that other factors such as the amount of time between trials do not change. When using real-world tasks, it is often difficult to administer tasks in a random order as easily as in a blocked order. By turning this job over to the computer, the researcher can be more certain that the only difference between two experimental groups is the practice schedule. An added bonus is that data are automatically and accurately recorded.

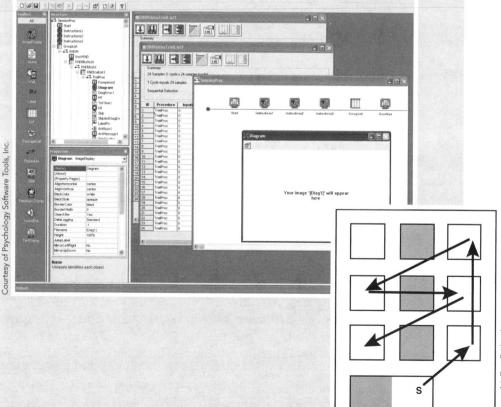

Courtesy of Psychology Software Tools, Inc.

Courtesy of Jeffrey Fairbrother.

distributed practice—A practice schedule in which the time that passes between successive trials of a task is usually longer than the time required to complete the task. Distributed practice also refers to situations in which practice is spread across several sessions.

choose to have a single training day lasting for 4 hours instead of asking employees to practice for 1 hour on four different days. A **distributed practice** schedule is one in which the rest between trials is longer than the amount of time it takes to complete a trial. In the rifle shooting example, the learner might have 15 seconds after shooting to begin sighting the next target. In the restaurant example, a schedule of 1-hour training sessions on four separate days would be a distributed schedule.

The distinction between massed and distributed practice schedules is an important one because all practice settings are limited by the amount of time available. Our tendency sometimes is to think that more practice is better even if it means that we need to pack it all into a tight schedule. Consider, for example, golfers hitting balls at a driving range. It is quite common to see them rapidly working their way through upward of 100 balls in a very short amount of time. Limited time creates a trade-off between the number of practice trials or sessions that can be completed and the amount of time that passes between these trials and sessions. In physical therapy settings, for example, patients are usually limited by their insurance company to a set number of office visits for a given condition. If the patient needs to strengthen her rotator cuff muscles, she will probably need to learn several exercises that she has never done before. Because correct technique is important, some proportion of her sessions should be devoted to teaching her these exercise skills. The therapist has to decide if it is perhaps better to devote the entire first day to practicing the skills and delay other activities such as massage, muscle stimulation, and ultrasound (i.e., a massed schedule) or to spend a smaller amount of time practicing the skills during several sessions (i.e., a distributed schedule) and devote the remainder of time in each session to other therapeutic activities.

When designing instructional experiences, there are several reasons to prefer a distributed practice schedule. First, there is evidence that massed practice can actually degrade learning (Lee & Genovese, 1988). This may happen in some skills because the massing procedure causes enough fatigue that the learner changes the way she executes the skill. Let's use the example of a swimmer working on keeping her elbow high during the recovery phase of her front crawl stroke (i.e., when she lifts her arm from the water to move it forward). There is a good chance that a massed schedule will cause her to start dropping her elbow as she gets fatigued. At this point, she will no longer be practicing the skill in the way she wants to learn it. In fact, she might just reinforce the poor technique she is trying to overcome. If she uses a distributed schedule instead, she will have a better chance of learning how to complete the movement correctly.

A second reason to prefer distributed practice is that massed practice sessions may not give the learner enough time to actually learn the skill. This could be especially true when training is presented in only one day. Learning is typically assessed after some delay following the completion of practice. So, a learner's performance at the end of a single day of training is not a good indication of the amount actually learned. Imagine that the physical therapist in the earlier example decided to devote just the first day to teaching the patient correct exercise technique. Because this is probably not enough time to learn these skills, the patient will be performing subsequent sessions using improper form unless she is closely supervised. It is also likely that she will come to depend on this supervision and will never really learn how to complete the exercises correctly. For this reason, on the first day, the therapist would probably instruct the patient, give her feedback when she needed it, and then physically guide her movements to ensure correct technique when she became fatigued. The therapist might start out subsequent sessions by "testing" the patient, monitoring her throughout the session, and correcting her as needed. After several sessions, there is a good chance that the patient will have learned the skills well enough to complete her exercises at home. During subsequent sessions, the therapist can quickly check the patient's technique and then devote more time to other interventions (e.g., ultrasound, flexibility training, or massage therapy).

A third reason to prefer distributed practice is that the fatigue caused by massing can increase the risk of injury in some activities. Some skills are inherently dangerous. Pole vaulting and many moves in gymnastics, for example, place athletes in extremely vulnerable positions. Other skills require training in dangerous environments. For example, firefighters train in burning structures, and military personnel are often surrounded by relative novices with live ammunition in their weapons. Although both firefighting and weapons training ultimately require that the trainee learn to perform well when tired or under stress, such conditions are typically introduced only when the aim is to transfer already learned skills to more realistic performance settings. Firefighters do sometimes need to drag hose lines up the stairs of a burning building after working hard for many consecutive hours, but these are not the conditions in which they first learn the skills required to perform this task.

Deciding How to Design Practice

The decision to use any given practice schedule should be based on the skill level of the learner, the demands of the task, and the eventual performance setting. Random practice can present an overwhelming challenge if a learner is relatively unskilled. For example, a novice tennis player might not be able to get into position quickly enough to practice forehands, backhands, and volleys in a random fashion. Instead, this player might initially benefit from blocked practice as she learns the complex patterns of coordination required for each stroke.

- Starting out with a blocked schedule seems to be particularly helpful for younger learners. Children are often not developmentally advanced enough to deal successfully with task demands. A tennis court, for example, offers relatively more ground to cover for an 8-year old than for an adult.
- As the learner gains proficiency, the instructor should begin to use random practice schedules if the task and performance setting will eventually require the performer to recall multiple tasks from memory.

⭐ **SUCCESS STORY**

John Wooden, UCLA Men's Basketball Coach

John Wooden is widely acclaimed as one of the best college basketball coaches of all time. During his 12 years at the University of California at Los Angeles (UCLA), his teams won 10 national championships. Coach Wooden earned a bachelor's degree in English from Purdue University and then served as basketball coach and athletic director at Indiana State Teacher's College (while also earning a master's degree). After college, Wooden played professional basketball and then went on to coach at both the high school and college levels. One of the characteristics that set Wooden apart from many other coaches was his approach to designing practices. He spent an enormous amount of time preparing for each practice session (sometimes more time than the practice itself lasted), and he took detailed notes about what happened during each practice. In his book describing his UCLA offense (Wooden & Nater, 1996), he indicated that his approach to skill instruction was based on what he called the "four laws of learning": (1) demonstration and instruction, (2) imitation, (3) correction, and (4) repetition. These laws echo many of the principles outlined in this book. Many of Wooden's practice drills were designed not only to teach certain plays but also to simulate the demands his players would face in a real game. In his descriptions of plays and drills, he also presented teaching points that included specific cues to help coaches implement the drills and identify common mistakes. These teaching points show that Wooden was aware of the instructional needs of both players and coaches learning his system.

AJ Mast/Icon SMI

- Varied practice should be used when the task and performance setting will require the learner to scale to the speed, force, or amplitude of his movement patterns. For example, an artist needs to learn how to select the correct amount of force to apply when painting. To transfer more paint to a canvas, a relatively large amount of force will be needed; to create very fine details, a relatively small amount of force will be needed.

- Constant practice can be used for those tasks that are performed the same way every time (e.g., a free throw shot), but it is important to recognize that such stable conditions are the exception rather than the rule in most real-world performance settings.

- Distributed practice schedules should be the first choice, but skilled performers might complete some practice under massed conditions if the eventual performance setting will require a similar effort. A skilled runner, for example, should have some experience in practicing correct stride technique while fatigued. Some form of massed practice may also be needed to train assembly line workers who have a limited amount of time between tasks.

A good rule of thumb to use when designing practice for any motor skill is to devote a portion of time to practicing in ways that resemble what occurs in the real-world performance setting. In sport, this can be accomplished by *scrimmaging.* For other movement activities, such as learning to button a shirt after losing the use of one hand, the instructor should identify the demands that the learner will face in an actual performance setting and try to duplicate them as closely as possible. For example, the person should wear the shirt so that the button and the hole are oriented in a realistic way. This idea is similar to the *dress rehearsals* that actors complete before opening a play. Dress rehearsals or scrimmages can provide a great opportunity to test a learner's skills. But because players in competitive simulations (e.g., scrimmages) often focus on outcomes (e.g., winning), overusing these types of drills during practice can cause learners to rely mostly on their strengths while neglecting their weaker skills. This situation can become even more pronounced in team sports, in that a focus on winning a scrimmage might mean that only the best players get any meaningful practice at all.

 I played just like at practice and that was the right recipe.

Roger Federer

With a little bit of planning, the instructor can use rehearsals to systematically test the skills of the learner to identify aspects of the skill that may need more practice. Once these weaknesses have been identified, the instructor might then decide to set up targeted practice drills using some of the practice schedules discussed earlier. For example, a piano teacher might decide that a student needs to spend some time in constant practice to work on a commonly used transition from one hand position to another. After this targeted practice, the instructor would once again test the student with a rehearsal by having her play music in which the transition occurs.

The Short of It

- Constant practice is appropriate when the task that is learned will always be performed in the same way. At times, limited use of constant practice can be helpful for introducing a learner to a new skill.
- Varied practice helps learners develop the capability to scale the speed, force, and amplitude of skills within a single class of movements (i.e., those that share an overall movement pattern such as an overhand throw).

- Blocked practice enhances performance during practice, but random practice enhances long-term learning. Blocked practice can be appropriate for children or new learners, or when tasks are difficult. Otherwise, random practice is preferred.
- Distributed practice is preferred to massed practice because it generally produces superior learning. Massed practice can be appropriate if it is needed to mimic the real-world demands of a skill.

CHAPTER 8

Putting It All Together: The Motor Skill Learning Cycle

Sacramento Bee/Zuma Press/Icon SMI

In this chapter you will learn the following:

✓ The phases and steps of the motor skill learning cycle

✓ How to consider the influence that the learner, the task, and the performance setting have on the design of instruction

✓ How to plan for practice by using the principles of motor behavior to create an effective practice design

✓ How to implement a practice plan that involves measuring performance, delivering feedback, and assessing learning

The concepts of *demands* and *resources* provide a conceptual framework for human factors. Demands and resources can come from the task, the device, the user, and the environment.

Neville Stanton (1997)

In the opening scenario for chapter 1, I asked you to imagine how you would select people to join a training program. I put this in the context of the dilemma faced by the United States during World War II as it searched for the best way to identify candidates for pilot training. Now that you have a much greater knowledge of the principles of motor behavior, I will ask you to take the next step and consider how to prepare a training program. Imagine you are an instructor in an outdoor recreation program and you will be conducting an afternoon instructional session for students wanting to learn some basic mountain biking skills (e.g., effective turning, hill descent, and riding over small obstacles). Your students will all know how to ride and will have their own bikes. They need to learn some specific bike control techniques so they can ride trails better. How will you plan the afternoon's activities? What do you need to know about your students? What sorts of activities could you use and how will you decide which ones to include? How will you measure their skills and interact with them?

These are the types of issues that all practitioners face when designing instructional activities. As the instructor in our mountain biking example, you will need to consider each student's previous experience with the skills you plan to teach. You will also need to find a suitable location that allows the students to practice the skills. You will need to find effective ways to introduce each skill. Will you simply demonstrate hill descent, or show a short video, or start by asking your students to shift their weight as a partner holds the bike steady? You will need to measure your students' performance in ways that allow you to give them appropriate feedback and provide you with the information you need to evaluate their progress. For example, what criteria will you use to assess their turning technique?

■   ■   ■

Now that you have learned about the ways in which motor behavior is studied (chapter 3), how we control our movements (chapter 4), how we learn movement skills (chapter 5), some of our basic capabilities and limitations related to motor skills (chapter 6), and the various ways of designing practice structures (chapter 7), you can begin to consider how you might apply this knowledge to create an effective instructional strategy when helping people to learn motor skills. Here is an overview of the four phases involved in the motor skill learning cycle and the steps in each of the first three phases (figure 8.1):

1. Consider the person, task, and performance setting.
   a. Identify important characteristics of the learner.
   b. Identify task demands.
   c. Identify ways in which the performance setting might influence the learner's attempts to meet task demands.
2. Plan for practice.
   a. Set learning goals.
   b. Develop instructions and demonstrations.
   c. Develop practice structure.
3. Implement practice.
   a. Measure performance.
   b. Provide feedback to the learner.
   c. Assess learning.
4. Review the overall instructional process.

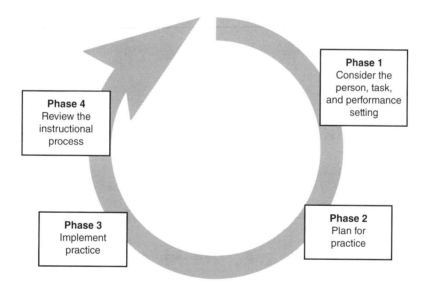

FIGURE 8.1 **The motor skill learning cycle.**

These phases and their steps represent a cyclical process that is repeated as a learner progresses. Each time through the cycle will be a little bit different than the previous times because the instructor will modify his or her approach in response to changes in the learner. As we look at the cycle, it is important to recognize that the order of certain steps may not always be the same as indicated in the list. For example, it might make sense to set learning goals before identifying the demands of the task. In other cases, some steps will be completed together when this makes sense, for example when the instructor develops special instructions for certain practice schedules. Certain steps will always occur in a set order. For example, measurement always occurs before feedback because the feedback is based on the information that comes from the measurement. The final step will normally be completed after one full cycle of the other steps. This is when the instructor will reflect on ways to improve the implementation of the instructional process represented by the cycle. After the cycle has been completed a number of times, it is likely that the instructor will continuously monitor the learning process. In the remainder of this chapter, I will discuss some examples of issues to consider in each of the steps of the cycle.

Phase 1: Consider the Person, Task, and Performance Setting

In the introduction to part II of this book, I indicated that one of the basic themes of the book is a concern for understanding the person, the task, and the performance setting related to any particular movement activity. One of the first steps to complete in the motor skill learning cycle is identifying the characteristics of the learner that will affect instructional decisions.

Identify Important Characteristics of the Learner

As you think about the learner, you should consider things such as the person's age, gender, previous experience, knowledge, skill level, capacity to process information, body type (height, weight, etc.), fitness (strength, speed, power, endurance, and flexibility), motivation, mental skills, injuries, and disabilities. This list could include almost an infinite number of characteristics, so it is important to think about which ones will influence the ways the learner works to meet the specific task demands of the skill being learned, as well as the ways the instructor designs the instructional setting to help the learner.

Consider dance training for 3- and 4-year-olds entering their first dance class compared to training for high school students who have been dancing for over 10 years. For the preschoolers, the instructor will choose activities that focus on basic movements. For example, an activity might be designed to teach the children to jump straight up in the air and land on two feet at the same time. This instructor will probably rely quite heavily on quick demonstrations because very young children cannot follow detailed instructions. It is also likely that the instructor will not spend a great deal of time having children practice any one activity, but will instead use variety to keep the children engaged. For the high school dancers, the instructor will tailor activities that fit the students' deeper knowledge and higher skill levels related to dance. For example, this instructor might spend a substantial amount of time teaching a complicated leap such as a grand jeté, focusing on the students' arm, hand, toe, shoulder, and head positions.

One way to identify important learner characteristics is to consider the capabilities and limitations that I outlined in chapter 6 and to think about how they might vary from one person to another. For example, we know that we all have the capability to process information from the environment and use it to help us control our movements. Now, let's consider how people might differ in this regard and what such differences would mean for an instructor trying to help a particular learner. Remember that the time it takes to process information can be drastically reduced when a person is in a situation that allows anticipation (Schmidt & Wrisberg, 2008). Because effective anticipation is based upon a body of knowledge regarding what to expect in a given situation, the various factors that influence our level of knowledge will influence our capability to anticipate, and this in turn will influence how long it takes to process information.

For example, when driving a car in traffic, most of us have enough experience and knowledge to anticipate many of the actions of other drivers. Think about how overwhelming it was for you the first time you drove on a crowded freeway. One of the reasons a situation like this is so stressful is that you do not know what to expect, and so you constantly try to monitor every detail you can in order to be able to react if needed. Such a strategy places a tremendous burden on your attentional capacity and requires a great deal of cognitive effort. Because the consequences of a mistake can be quite large, it makes sense that you would have an elevated stress level when engaged in a task that you feel you cannot quite keep up with. As you gain more experience, knowledge, and skill, you learn to anticipate actions and learn that you can monitor a relatively small set of cues to effectively understand what is happening around you.

> *[Bruce Lee] related everything to a personal basis, taking into consideration a person's height, speed, and so on. Some people kicked fast, others slow, some were better with their hands. So he taught each man to find out his own strengths and to use them. He taught everyone to recognize his own weaknesses, too.*
>
> **Danny Inosanto (Lee & Bleecker, 1989)**

From an instructional standpoint, experience, knowledge, and skill are important considerations. When first teaching someone to drive, instructors typically try to simplify the environment by using an empty parking lot so that learners can focus all of their attention on learning the basic ways to control the car. As the learner gains proficiency, the instructor gradually introduces more realistic demands such as driving on roads and then driving in light traffic. This example shows how the characteristics of the learner (in this case, experience, knowledge, and skill) can influence the decisions an instructor makes. The bottom line is that we want to tailor our instruction to the needs of the individual learner to the extent we can. The only way we can do this is to take the time to identify the important characteristics of the learner that will influence the way we approach instruction.

Identify Task Demands

Another important step in designing instruction involves considering the demands that the skill or skills to be learned will place on the performer. One way of accomplishing this is to ask questions such as these:

- Does the skill emphasize decision making?
- Is there a limited amount of time to respond?
- Are the cues for decision making hard to detect?
- How complex is the skill?
- Is the skill rapid and discrete (e.g., passing a basketball) or slow and continuous (e.g., dribbling)?
- Is anticipation possible?
- What sources of sensory information are used?
- Are any speed–accuracy trade-offs involved?
- Does the skill require precise timing or the coordination of multiple limbs?
- Can the skill be broken down into steps?

When we consider complex real-world skills, the list of task demands can become extremely long. The idea is to focus on the demands that are most important for a particular learner given a specific performance setting. In chapter 3, you read about the *closed* and *open* skill classification scheme. You probably remember that *open skills* are those performed in a changing and sometimes unpredictable environment. In other words, they force the learner to adapt to changing situations. This type of demand requires the learner to develop skills related to decision making and, if possible, anticipation. So, practice should be designed with this in mind. It is a fairly common practice procedure to simplify open skills by removing the decision-making component, as when a baseball is placed on a tee. This can be an appropriate technique as long as the instructor remembers that the learner needs to eventually learn how to deal with the decision-making demands of hitting a moving ball in the ultimate performance setting.

Another example can be seen in most rehabilitation settings. Because patients are obviously vulnerable to injury, rehabilitation exercises are typically conducted in fairly controlled and predictable environments. For example, a person recovering her capability to walk after an auto accident needs to focus on the basics of maintaining her balance and learning to complete her step cycles adequately. At this point, she does not need the added demand of navigating around other moving people or avoiding unexpected obstacles. For this reason, the clinical setting is typically designed to allow the patient to work on regaining basic function without any other demands. As the patient recovers her strength and walking skills, the therapist will probably begin to reintroduce some real-world demands by asking her to walk in a hallway or some other location where she might encounter just a few other people or objects.

Identify Influences of the Performance Setting

As the instructor considers the demands of the task, he or she will probably also start to think about how these demands are influenced by the performance setting. For example, consider a surgeon completing an operation. Time pressure for the completion of a suture may not be an issue under normal circumstances, but it will become an issue if the suture is suddenly needed to stop excessive bleeding.

SUCCESS STORY

Damian Farrow, Australian Institute of Sport

Damian Farrow began his university studies at Deakin University, where he received a bachelor's degree in physical education and subsequently a master's degree in skill acquisition. He finished his studies at the University of Queensland, earning a doctorate in motor expertise. Damian started his career as a physical education teacher and tennis coach before taking a lecturing position in the School of Human Movement and Sports Science at the University of Ballarat. In 2002, Damian became the inaugural skill acquisition specialist at the Australian Institute of Sport, where he is currently the acting head of the Psychology and Skill Acquisition Discipline. Working directly with coaches, he and his staff employ the principles of motor behavior to help Australia's national teams implement effective skill instruction designs. He has a particular interest in helping athletes develop their decision-making and perceptual skills. He has worked with a wide variety of Australian national teams and development programs including netball, water polo, cricket, rugby, Australian football, swimming, and tennis. Damian also conducts applied research on various aspects of sport performance. He has completed studies examining techniques to train anticipation and perceptual skills, the effects of different practice schedules on learning sport skills, and attentional demands in sport. One of his most influential papers (Farrow & Abernethy, 2002) presented the results of a study demonstrating how video training and implicit learning can help tennis players effectively anticipate serve direction.

Photo courtesy of Damian Farrow.

You have likely experienced a more common example of how the setting can influence performance. When you drive on a relatively uncrowded highway, the primary demand you face is to keep your car in the center of your lane. When you instead drive in heavy traffic in a city, you encounter a much more demanding setting that requires you to monitor several other vehicles, continually change the speed of your car, and make decisions about how to change lanes or avoid erratic drivers.

The performance setting affects more than just the task demands, however. It can also have a pronounced effect on the performer as he tries to meet the task demands. One clear example of this occurs when individuals have difficulty performing because of the presence of an audience. For many people, performing in front of others elevates their arousal level to such an extent that they no longer perform at their best. But this does not always have to be the case. Coaches often look for ways to "reframe" their athletes' interpretation of a setting to counteract potential problems related to arousal. Consider the story of the 1954 Indiana state high school basketball champions, the Milan Indians (the movie *Hoosiers* was based on this team). Milan was an extremely small town, and the coach recognized that his players would understandably be intimidated playing in a larger arena during the finals. To reassure his athletes, the coach measured the height of the goal in the large arena to illustrate that it was the same height as in every other court (Sports Hollywood, 2007). Observation by others also occurs outside of competitive sport settings, as when a supervisor watches an employee, friends watch each other in a recreational sport, a physical education student performs in front of classmates, or a musician plays during a recital.

Performance settings can differ from practice settings in several other ways that might influence the performer or the task demands (or both). These differences might include changes in the physical aspects of the setting (e.g., equipment, facilities, or weather) or the presence of additional demands on the performer's attention. Unforeseen changes in equipment or facilities can have devastating effects on performance. On the day before the pole vault event during the 1972 Summer Olympics, certain poles were banned from the competition. As a result, the U.S. team was not allowed to compete with the poles they had used during training. Many athletes and coaches in the pole-vaulting community believe that this factor contributed to the failure of the United States to win the gold medal for the first time in modern Olympic history (J. Bemiller, personal communication, February 14, 2008). The weather in the performance setting can also influence performance. Pilots of certain aircraft need to be certified in flying using only instruments so that they can fly safely when cloud cover lowers visibility.

Skill Insight

There are several distinct ways in which we can commit errors during motor performance (Reason, 1990). Errors can be divided into two general categories; one is related to planning, and the other is related to execution. When we plan a movement, we might mistakenly decide on an action that will not accomplish our goal. There is a mismatch between our goal and our understanding of how we can achieve it. For example, a person just learning archery might think she is aiming for the center of the target, but fail to account for the effects that wind and gravity will have on the arrow as it flies. The second category of errors includes what have been called *slips* and *lapses*. A slip occurs when our execution does not meet our goal even though we planned the movement correctly. For example, when painting a wall near a window or door, you plan to keep the brush away from the molding but sometimes have a *slip of the brush*. A lapse is less obvious and may be detected only by the performer. Lapses generally result from a failure of memory during a movement. I often experience a lapse when I drive my wife's car; her windshield wiper control works in the exact opposite direction of the one in my car. I know that in her car I should move the lever up, but when I perform the movement I sometimes forget this and instead perform the action that is correct for my car.

Even very subtle changes in the performance setting can introduce attentional demands that influence performance. Have you ever noticed that when you are running late you tend to make mistakes? It may be that because you are devoting so much attention to remembering everything you need to do, you don't have enough attention left to actually complete the tasks you are trying to accomplish. The mistakes I commonly make include not pushing the refrigerator door with enough force to close it, missing the light switch, and completely forgetting to do things such as putting my coffee cup into the dishwasher.

Thinking about how the performance setting will influence task demands and the performer is an important step when one is formulating an instructional plan. Some of the features of a performance setting can be foreseen, and so the instructor can design practice activities to prepare learners for this situation. For example, the physical therapist helping his patient to walk again knows that eventually the skill will be completed in settings that involve covering uneven ground and avoiding obstacles and other people. Although it is not always possible to know the exact circumstances in which a skill will be performed, instructors still can use general ideas to help learners prepare. American football coaches know that their players will have to play in extreme temperatures (hot and cold) and will have to perform on different surfaces (natural or artificial). Surgery instructors know that their students will have to perform under time pressure, react to unexpected events, and at times may even operate in substandard conditions (e.g., in a field setting). Your driver's training instructor knew that you would need to learn how to drive in traffic. A good approach to instruction will incorporate performance in settings that simulate the demands the learner will likely face in the real world.

Phase 2: Plan for Practice

During phase 2, the practitioner develops a strategy for providing assistance to the learner. This is when plans are made for how practice sessions will actually be carried out. The information from phase 1 is an essential part of the planning process.

Set Learning Goals

In almost all cases, the learner should be involved in setting goals. When learners are involved in choosing their goals, they are typically more motivated to engage in the practice activities (Locke & Latham, 1985). There are several important considerations in setting learning goals. The practitioner and learner should identify specific short-term and long-term goals relevant to the motor skills to be learned. A short-term goal for a fashion design student learning to use a sewing machine might be to sew an even stitch along a curved line. A long-term goal might be to sew an entire outfit for a term project in a design class. When setting goals, the practitioner and learner should focus on goals that will be both challenging and realistic for the learner. Because goals tell us how to direct our efforts, it is important to consider different types of goals (Schmidt & Wrisberg, 2008). Some goals focus on the *process* or *technique* of the movement. Examples of performers setting

process goal—A learning goal that focuses on the technique or form of a movement.

outcome goal—A learning goal that focuses on the outcome that results from a movement.

process goals include a gymnast wanting to hold her body in better alignment during a handstand, a surfer wanting to get to his feet quicker once he catches a wave, a dancer wanting to complete the correct sequence of steps for a new routine, and a surgeon wanting to tie higher-quality sutures. Other goals focus on the *outcome* or *end result* of the movement. Examples of performers setting **outcome goals** include a gymnast wanting to receive a score of 10 on a floor routine, a surfer wanting to win his heat in a competition, a dancer wanting to be selected to a stage show based on an audition performance, and a surgeon wanting to reduce the amount of time it takes to tie a set of sutures in a particular procedure.

In learning situations, goals are often stated in relative terms. A relative goal indicates how a learner wants to improve her motor skills with respect to her current level of proficiency. The focus is on improvement to a skill level beyond the level that a learner currently possesses. In the examples I just gave for process goals, this type of improvement was indicated by my use of terms such as "better" and "quicker." Stating goals in relative terms can be helpful if it directs attention to aspects of the performance that are under the learner's control. Stating a goal in relative terms might also be motivating because it emphasizes the learner's progress. In contrast, stating a goal in absolute terms (e.g., receiving a perfect score in a diving competition) might undermine motivation if it continually reinforces a message of insufficient performance. But it is important to recognize that how a learner reacts to a goal will depend as much on the individual learner as on how the goal is stated. Some people may be extremely motivated by ambitious goals stated in an absolute fashion. A lack of progress might just strengthen their resolve. The important idea is for practitioners to be aware of the different potential effects of goal setting so that the instructional decisions can be made to best serve the individual needs of the learner.

Develop Instructions and Demonstrations

Instructions are an integral part of any type of practice. Instructions for motor skills are typically presented verbally by a practitioner. Common examples include a coach instructing an athlete or a physical educator teaching a student. Sometimes instructions are presented in written form or as a combination of pictures and written text. Knot-tying instructions are commonly presented in a series of pictures with written descriptions of the steps. In most cases, however, verbal instructions are supplemented by a demonstration of the skill to be learned. Demonstrations might be performed by the practitioner, a skilled performer, or a learner, and can be presented in person or through a format such as videotape. Recently, video instruction and demonstration have become quite common on Web sites such as YouTube.

Instructions should be developed with a few important ideas in mind. First, to be effective, instructions should match the learning goals, especially with respect to the specific actions the learner is supposed to take. This may seem obvious, but it is not uncommon for rather vague goals (e.g., "I want to get better") to be paired with specific instructions directing the learner to focus on only a small part of the activity to be learned (e.g., working only on a follow-through movement). Similarly, very specific goals (for example, "I want to become a 70 percent free throw shooter") are sometimes paired with generic instructions (e.g., "Keep practicing" or "Shoot more free throws"). Both of these examples are far from ideal. In the first example, the instruction might help the learner get better on only one aspect of the performance when the goal is overall improvement. In the second example, the instructions do not include enough specific direction to tell the learner how to achieve the goal.

Second, because attentional capacity is limited, instructions should be kept as brief as possible. Learners typically cannot keep track of lengthy and detailed instructions. This is particularly important to recognize when one is teaching young children or new learners. Third, instructions direct the learner's attention to specific aspects of the movement or environmental cues. For this reason, the practitioner should be careful to develop instructions that direct the learner's attention appropriately. At the very least, the practitioner should consider whether attention should be directed internally (e.g., to the feel of solid contact when driving a golf ball) or externally (e.g., to the location of the hole when putting). In addition, it is important to consider whether the learner has to focus on just a few things (e.g., as in a penalty kick in soccer) or on many things (e.g., as in dribbling a ball down the field against several defenders) Focus of attention is also important when it comes to demonstrations because learners typically need to be told which aspects of the demonstration are the important ones.

> *Everything was planned out each day. In fact, in my later years at UCLA I would spend two hours every morning with my assistants organizing that day's practice session (even though the practice itself might be less than two hours long).*
>
> **John Wooden (1997)**

Develop Practice Structure

In this step, the practitioner makes plans for how practices will be structured. He or she will decide when to use constant practice to focus on one skill per session and when to use varied practice to strengthen the schema for a skill that requires parameter variations. The practitioner will also decide if it is best to practice multiple skills in either a blocked or a random practice schedule. To do this effectively, he or she should give some consideration to the learner characteristics and task demands identified in earlier steps. Instructors will also decide the number of trials a learner will complete in each practice session and how much of a break will occur between trials. For some skills, not giving enough rest between trials can disrupt both performance and learning. The amount of time available for practice is often limited. This might mean that the practitioner needs to decide how many tasks to practice and how many trials to complete for each task in a 30- or 60-minute session. In other cases, a decision must be made about how to use a set amount of time each week. For example, if 6 hours a week are allotted to practice, would it be more effective to hold two 3-hour sessions, three 2-hour sessions, or six 1-hour sessions? In many cases, there is also some type of deadline for the completion of practice. In sport, practice is structured around the time available before deadlines set according to the opening of a season, the schedule of games, and travel demands. In a rehabilitation setting, the number of visits might be dictated by an insurance company. For other activities, a deadline might be established by a predefined course of instruction as is commonly seen in classes designed to teach skills in art, ceramics, music, and dance.

Other decisions about practice structure relate to the actual practice activities themselves. Depending upon the learner and the task demands, the practitioner might decide to use part practice instead of teaching skills in their entirety. The practitioner will also determine if and when it will be useful to use other types of practice such as observational learning, mental practice, and simulations, as well as how to measure performance, provide feedback, and assess learning.

Phase 3: Implement Practice

Once the practitioner has created a plan for practice, he or she will need to implement it. During the implementation, the practitioner will probably make several adjustments as he or she notes how well the implementation proceeds. With careful planning, however, major modifications will not be needed and in fact should be avoided. The reason is that a major change during practice makes it impossible to tell whether the learner's behavior was in response to the original implementation or to the change. It is best to try the original ideas long enough to get a solid idea of how well they work, then make any changes needed and test them in the same way so that comparisons can be made. In sport and physical education settings, implementing an effective practice session involves much more than "rolling out the balls." During any given practice session, practitioners need to introduce the activities with appropriate instructions, measure learners' performances, and provide feedback. In addition, some practice sessions will also have a portion of time devoted to assessing how much learning has actually occurred.

Measure Performance

The first consideration about measurement is that the type of measure used must match the learning goals that have been set. If process goals are pursued, then **process measures** should be used to measure performance. A process measure is one that provides information about the pattern of movement during the execution of a motor skill. For example, an overhand throw consists of a clearly coordinated pattern involving taking a step toward the target, stretching the throwing arm back, bringing the throwing arm forward, bringing the nonthrowing arm down and backward, and rotating the torso so that the shoulder of the throwing arm moves in the direction of the target. In many practical settings, process measures are

process measure—A measure of performance that focuses on movement technique or form.

simply observations by experienced practitioners who know how to subjectively evaluate the pattern of movement. However, one can also evaluate patterns of movement by capturing them on videotape for slow-motion or stop-motion replay. Video allows fairly precise measurement of the timing of events in a movement, which enables practitioners to pay close attention to sequencing of movements and the relative timing of each part of the movement with respect to other parts or to the whole action. For example, a common problem that children encounter with the overhand throw is coordinating the step with bringing the throwing arm forward. My 5-year-old daughter knows that both these elements are involved but will take a distinct step, stop completely, and then bring her arm forward. So, she has a general idea of the sequence of actions but has not learned the timing required.

If outcome goals are pursued, then **outcome measures** are appropriate. Remember that outcome goals are those that focus on the end result of the movement. Continuing with the overhand throw example, an outcome goal might be to throw the ball accurately enough so that the person catching it can do so without having to move too much. A more advanced outcome goal, for a baseball pitcher for example, might be to strike out a batter. Similar to process measures, outcome measures can sometimes involve fairly straightforward observation, as when you see a ball going into a goal or a patient successfully walking 10 steps without a cane. In other cases, outcome measures are provided by instruments. For example, in most newer cars a driver knows that the emergency brake is fully disengaged when he moves the handle to a point that closes an electronic switch and turns off a light on the instrument panel.

outcome measure—A measure of performance that focuses on the outcome that results from a movement.

Provide Feedback to the Learner

Once the learner's performance has been measured, feedback can be given if needed. The type of feedback I discuss in this section refers to information that is not readily available to the learner and so must be provided by an outside source. This source is typically a practitioner (e.g., a coach) or some type of device (e.g., a stopwatch). The consistency between the types of goals and measures that I outlined earlier continues with feedback. **Knowledge of performance** (KP) is the type of feedback to use when addressing process goals and measures because it is feedback regarding the pattern of the movement for a skill. Examples include a trainer telling a firefighter trainee to hold the hose with the nozzle in front, a physical educator telling a student to kick the ball harder, and an occupational therapist telling a patient recovering from a repetitive use injury to relax her shoulders when she uses the mouse on her computer. **Knowledge of results** (KR) is the type of feedback used when one is addressing outcome goals and measures because it refers to the end result of the movement. Examples include a runner reading her split times from a stopwatch, a gymnastics coach giving an athlete a score of 8 after a practice routine, and a physical therapist telling a patient that she completed six correct repetitions of an exercise.

knowledge of performance—Feedback provided to a learner that focuses on movement technique or form.

knowledge of results—Feedback provided to a learner that focuses on the outcome resulting from a movement.

Skill Insight

Learning can be enhanced by the withholding of feedback. This may seem a bit contrary to common experience, because teachers and coaches often seem to subscribe to a *more is better* philosophy when it comes to giving feedback. In fact, research on motor learning has shown that people sometimes learn better when they get feedback only after every other trial (Winstein & Schmidt, 1990). These studies suggest that providing feedback too often causes the learner to become dependent upon the instructor for evaluating a movement. Imagine that you are trying to learn to complete an overhand volleyball serve. If your coach always tells you what you did right or wrong, then you may stop trying to figure this out for yourself. Your learning, however, is dependent upon your efforts to figure out, for yourself, how the results of your actions matched your original intentions as well as what your movements *felt* like. It seems that we don't learn as well when we stop trying to interpret the results of our actions for ourselves.

Feedback can also be divided into two categories, known as prescriptive and descriptive. **Prescriptive feedback** statements tell the learner how to fix a problem. That is, they include some instruction for future attempts of the skill. All of the examples of KP that I gave previously were prescriptive. The directive "Keep your head down," so commonly heard in the game of golf, is another example of prescriptive feedback. **Descriptive feedback** statements simply describe what happened on a particular trial. A descriptive statement for the golf example might be "You topped the ball." Descriptive feedback assumes that the learner knows how to adjust his behavior after receiving the feedback. This type of feedback can be problematic for early learners because they often do not know what to correct. Accordingly, descriptive feedback should be used only when it is clear that the learner will know how to interpret and use it. Prescriptive feedback can also have drawbacks. Although it is very useful for new learners who need the additional instruction, it might become a distraction for individuals who know how to correct an error once they have been alerted to it.

prescriptive feedback—Feedback provided to the learner that includes instruction about how to improve performance on the next attempt.

descriptive feedback—Feedback provided to the learner that simply characterizes what happened in the performance.

Assess Learning

The final aspect of practice implementation involves the assessment of learning, what most of us think of as "testing." Assessment occurs when a practitioner measures performance after some delay with the purpose of determining how much a person has learned. This differs from observation of performance during practice, which does not necessarily tell the practitioner how well an individual has learned a given motor skill. Performance during practice can be influenced by temporary effects that can either improve or degrade a person's performance. For example, providing frequent feedback enhances performance for most motor skills. So, how a learner performs when receiving frequent feedback (which is often the case during practice) will not reveal how much she has actually learned. The most common way to assess learning is to give a test after a long enough time delay to allow any temporary effects to wear off. A one-day delay is frequently used in motor learning research, but a practitioner should choose the delay that makes the most sense for the skills being taught. For example, when athletic therapy students learn to perform a drawer test to detect ligament ruptures in the knee, they should not be tested right after practicing the procedure. Instead, a longer delay will provide a better picture of how well they will be able to perform this procedure after they have had time to forget some of the critical aspects of the skill. Those students who have actually learned the skill will forget less than those who have not learned it as well and will therefore perform better on a delayed test.

> *You know where you'd like to go, whether it's to a national championship in basketball or a particular goal in your business or life. You must also realize that this goal will be simply a by-product of all the hard work and good thinking you do along the way—your preparation.*
>
> **John Wooden (1997)**

For many skills, the ultimate "test" is when the skills are used in their intended real-world setting. For competitive activities in sport, music, or dance, the real-world test comes during competition or some other public performance. For other skills, such as those involved in surgery, dentistry, piloting an airplane, or driving a bus, the real-world test can have potentially serious consequences if the performer doesn't do well. So, for such real-world skills, practitioners should attempt to assess learning by replicating real-world demands as much as possible. In pilot training, for example, this is achieved through the use of sophisticated simulators. Whether a simulator is used or not, tests should mimic the demands of real-world settings whenever possible. One can usually incorporate assessments into practice sessions by devoting a set period of time to skill testing. These assessments should be administered near the beginning of the practice session before the day's practice can exert temporary effects on learners' performance.

Phase 4: Review the Overall Instructional Process

In the final phase of the motor skill learning cycle, the practitioner reviews each of the previous steps and considers how effective the instructional strategy has been. This phase is actually an ongoing process. That is, the practitioner continually reflects on his instructional decisions and attempts to evaluate how well the current efforts are working. I introduce this as the final phase because this type of review and assessment is best done after a fairly stable history of instruction has been established. Frequently changing the elements of the motor skill learning cycle before there is an adequate baseline of experience with learners often undermines the practitioner's effectiveness. Changing an instructional approach too often makes it hard to tell what parts were working and what parts weren't. The basic idea is that the practitioner should always be aware of ways to improve an instructional approach, but should think carefully about when to make changes. For example, a soccer coach might review her approach periodically during a season based on the team's performance and make minor modifications, but should definitely reflect on what did and did not work once the season has ended.

The Short of It

- The first phase of the motor skill learning cycle requires the practitioner to consider the characteristics of the learner, the demands of the task, and the ways in which the performance setting will influence both the learner and the task demands.
- The second phase of the cycle involves planning practice sessions by identifying goals, developing instructions and demonstrations, and deciding on which practice schedules to use.
- The third phase of the cycle focuses on implementing the practice plan in a way that allows the practitioner to measure performance, provide effective feedback, and assess learning.
- The fourth and final phase of the cycle occurs when the practitioner reflects on how well a given approach has worked and decides what sorts of changes might be needed to improve future practice experiences.

The Future of Motor Behavior

> The best way to predict the future is to create it.
>
> **Peter Drucker**

Despite all we know about motor behavior, there are many questions that are still unanswered. As you apply the information in this book, it is important to remember that some research is fairly definitive. For example, it is well established that the capability to successfully anticipate an event will reduce the amount of time required to respond to that event. Performance in sports that require rapid responses can almost always benefit from anticipation training. The trick is to identify the relevant information that can be used for advanced decision making. In some cases, research has given us ideas about what information is important. In receiving a tennis serve, for example, skilled players tend to gather early information by looking at the movements of their opponent's head, shoulders, and trunk (Williams et al., 2002). Less skilled players wait until later during the serve to gather information from the server's racket and ball motion.

Sometimes, we have what might be called *generally useful principles* that give us some direction when we consider how a person can try to meet the demands of a task in certain performance settings. Because each of these three factors (person, task, and setting) has many dimensions, the combinations that are created by their interactions are essentially limitless. So, experienced professionals might test how well a principle applies to their specific instructional needs before adopting a given practice activity based on the principle. For example, we know that in general the faster you move the less accurate you will be. There are, however, exceptions to this principle. It turns out that very rapid movements requiring a large proportion of the total force we can generate can sometimes be accomplished more accurately when we speed up. In chapter 6, I illustrated this idea with the example of chopping wood with an axe. Because this task requires you to swing fast in the first place, swinging even faster might improve your accuracy. There are many activities, however, that have yet to be studied thoroughly. We don't know, for example, if serving a tennis ball harder (i.e., faster) will improve accuracy or not. Many recreational players I've spoken with believe that players need to slow down to preserve serving accuracy. This is why these players say their second serves (i.e., after a bad first serve) are typically slower than first serves. Although speed–accuracy trade-offs are among the most widely researched issues in motor behavior, there is actually still much to be learned about how they affect performance in real-world settings. Incidentally, high-level tennis players often use a different type of serve after they default on the first one, so a comparison of serving speed is not always useful for these athletes.

Looking to the future of motor behavior, we see many exciting topics that still need to be addressed. Many of these questions relate to how well the basic principles we've discovered in the laboratory will work in real-world settings. Because real-world settings involve a variety of complex interactions between the person, task, and setting, the results from controlled experiments don't always translate directly to practical settings. Problems stemming from this fact are a part of the challenge that practitioners face when implementing evidence-based instruction. These efforts will be helped by more studies that offer comprehensive descriptions of how people perform specific tasks. For example, only one research study has examined the skills required in the sport of surfing (Fairbrother & Boxell, 2008). Future efforts in the study of surfing skills will be facilitated if we first have good descriptions of how skilled (and less skilled) surfers perform basic maneuvers.

We should also expect to see some exciting interdisciplinary collaborations. The increased use of imaging devices that have been developed to study the brain and nervous system will likely broaden our understanding of brain function as it relates to motor control and learning. Recent work in this area has shown that simply reading a text passage about a hockey game activates the same areas of the brain that are used when planning a movement (Saunders, 2008). Other collaborations between researchers studying the various dimensions of human behavior should help us develop a richer understanding of the multiple factors that shape of motor performance in different settings. For example, some researchers in motor development have recently noted that levels of physical activity may be tied to how well people develop fundamental motor skills during childhood (Stodden et al., 2008). This suggests that future research targeted at understanding the current obesity epidemic will include the efforts of researchers who study motor behavior, as well those who are interested in nutrition, physiology, and psychology.

The future of motor behavior will likely be tied to advances in technology. As high-speed video and other motion analysis devices become more widely available, we will start to see them used more frequently in real-world settings. This will help practitioners and researchers address practical problems and document the effective patterns of movement used by individuals in a wide variety of activities. Documenting effective patterns will help us determine whether or not instruction based on conventional wisdom is correct. In the surfing study I mentioned earlier, one of the important things we found was that a widely held belief about how surfers move from the prone position to their feet was in fact not a very good reflection of what the surfers actually did. For the vast majority of movement skills, we simply don't know how well our currently accepted instructional techniques work.

Another interesting area that might receive increasing attention in the future relates to how learners change across time. Currently, we don't have a very detailed picture of how a person changes—behaviorally, neurologically, or otherwise—during the course of a long-term learning experience. Most of our understanding of skill development in adults is based on comparisons between groups of people who possess different levels of skills. However, recognizing the differences between expert and novice acrobats, for example, does not necessarily tell us *how* a person moves from a novice juggler to a member of Cirque du Soleil.

What Will You Do?

Now that we are at the end of this book, it is time for me to ask you: What will you do? I hope that in addition to introducing you to motor behavior, this book has inspired you to continue to learn about how humans control their movements and learn motor skills. As I tried to illustrate in chapter 2 and with numerous examples throughout the book, there are many professional paths to follow when one is applying this knowledge. Will you pursue a doctorate in one of the subfields of motor behavior? Will you become a coach or a physical educator? Will you become an athletic trainer, physical therapist, or occupational therapist? Perhaps you will do none of these but will become a well-informed parent who uses your knowledge of motor behavior to support your children as they learn movement skills. Human movement is such an important part of life! And I hope you agree by now that there are many ways to apply the principles of motor behavior to help people improve their movement skills. I wish you the best of luck as you pursue your chosen professional path.

Appendix A

Learn More About Motor Behavior

Books

▶ Haywood, K.M., & Getchell, N. (2009). *Life Span Motor Development,* Fifth Edition. Champaign, IL: Human Kinetics.

An introductory college text on motor development.

▶ Magill, R.A. (2007). *Motor Learning and Control: Concepts and Applications,* Eighth Edition. New York: McGraw-Hill.

Written for undergraduate college students, this book focuses on introducing concepts related to motor learning and control and on discussing the application of these concepts to various motor skill learning or performance situations.

▶ Rosenbaum, D.A. (1991). *Human Motor Control.* San Diego: Academic Press.

A graduate-level or advanced-undergraduate introduction to motor control.

▶ Schmidt, R.A., & Lee, T.D. (2005). *Motor Control and Learning: A Behavioral Emphasis,* Fourth Edition. Champaign, IL: Human Kinetics.

An advanced graduate-level textbook on motor behavior that offers comprehensive details on research in motor learning and control. It also presents an excellent history of motor behavior research.

▶ Schmidt, R.A., & Wrisberg, C.A. (2008). *Motor Learning and Performance: A Situation-Based Learning Approach,* Fourth Edition. Champaign, IL: Human Kinetics.

An excellent introductory text for undergraduate college students. It provides easy-to-read descriptions of the principles of motor behavior and discusses real-world applications.

▶ Vickers, J.N. (2007). *Perception, Cognition, and Decision Training: The Quiet Eye in Action.* Champaign, IL: Human Kinetics.

A good overview of research on how high-level performers control their gaze during the execution of motor skills. The book also provides a brief overview of important ideas from research in motor learning and control.

▶ Wrisberg, C.A. (2007). *Sport Skill Instruction for Coaches*. Champaign, IL: Human Kinetics.

A practical guide to help coaches implement principles of motor behavior and sport psychology in their work with athletes.

▶ Wulf, G. (2007). *Attention and Motor Skill Learning*. Champaign, IL: Human Kinetics.

A short book reviewing the research on how instructions to direct attention affect the performance and learning of motor skills.

Web Sites

▶ American Psychological Association, Division 47 (www.apa47.org)

Division 47 is focused primarily on sport psychology, but many research topics overlap with those of interest to researchers in motor behavior.

▶ Canadian Society for Psychomotor Learning and Sport Psychology (www.scapps.org)

Canadian organization devoted to promotion of the study of motor behavior and sport psychology. Its main focus is on the exchange of information among academic researchers.

▶ North American Society for the Psychology of Sport and Physical Activity (www.nasp-spa.org)

The primary international organization for researchers in the field of motor behavior.

Appendix B

Implementing Motor Behavior in the Real World

Athlete

☐ Incorporate skill training that emphasizes how you control your movements and the ways in which you learn this control.

☐ For sports requiring decision-making skills, identify the factors that influence the quality and speed of your decisions. For example, deciding whether to pass the ball or shoot in soccer depends upon the position of all the players on the field who can influence the play. In practice, create realistic scenarios that challenge your decision making.

☐ For sports that emphasize preparation and execution (e.g., archery), focus your practice on these elements of your performance. Identify what you currently do and reflect on what you did during moments of peak performance. Document how variations in your behavior affect your performance to identify which behaviors are supportive and which are problematic.

☐ Find a coach or a training partner who has expertise that you do not possess yourself and who is a skilled observer of the movements required by your sport. At the highest levels of performance, your relationship should be collaborative, which will allow you to control many of the aspects of your training while still receiving another knowledgeable person's perspective.

☐ Identify and use the appropriate type of feedback during practice. Do not become reliant on external feedback during practice. Learn to use the sensory information that is directly available to you as a result of your movements (e.g., how the movement felt to you) to connect your intended goal (what you wanted to do) with the outcome (what happened).

☐ Use a variety of practice techniques to take advantage of the different ways you learn. Challenge yourself to improve the skills that are relevant to competition in your sport. Remember that performance during practice does not reflect learning. Some types of practice (e.g., random practice schedules) can degrade your performance during practice but actually result in better learning (and better performance during competition).

☐ Be certain that the way you practice matches your performance goals in terms of the activities you complete, the way you measure your performance, and the feedback you receive.

Physical Educator

☐ Incorporate skill training into lesson plans to help your students develop fundamental motor skills and learn critical skills for sport and other movements so that they can engage in a lifetime of various physical activity pursuits.

☐ Consider the capabilities and limitations of your students as well as the skills they need to learn. This will help you identify the best approaches to teaching motor skills to your particular students. Elementary school children will most likely be learning fundamental motor skills and the basic rules of movement games. Secondary school students will spend more time learning complex real-world sport and movement skills (e.g., dance), as well as the rules and strategies associated with real-world sport and movement activities.

☐ Take advantage of positive transfer between movement skills by presenting the units for these skills in close proximity. For example, teaching badminton strokes by illustrating their similarities and differences with tennis strokes will be more effective if your students have recently completed a unit on tennis.

☐ Recognize the different ways in which your students learn and then design activities accordingly. So-called free play activities can be a way to take advantage of implicit learning if your students have mastered the basics of certain movement skills. For example, free play in soccer can implicitly reinforce dribbling, kicking, and passing skills. Observation of classmates can also facilitate learning, so those times when some students are waiting to participate need not be wasteful.

☐ Use an appropriate amount of specifically targeted feedback. Don't provide feedback too frequently. Instead, allow your students to develop their skill at using their own sensory information to self-evaluate their performances. Be certain that the feedback you give matches the learning goal and the way performance is measured.

☐ Allow your students to have some control over their learning experience. They can benefit from being allowed to decide when they want to receive feedback, additional instructions, or physical guidance.

☐ Use a variety of practice techniques to effectively challenge your students in ways that will benefit long-term retention of their motor skills.

Athletic Coach

☐ Incorporate skill training into practice sessions to help your athletes develop the effective movement techniques needed for their sport. Motor skill training encompasses the learning of movement control and coordination, as well as perceptual and cognitive skills needed to support performance.

☐ If your sport requires decision-making skills, identify the factors that influence the quality and speed of the decisions your athletes make. Do your athletes, for example, make the right decisions during practice but not under the pressure to respond rapidly in a game? To the extent that you can, be sure that practice replicates the demands that the athlete will face in competition.

☐ If your sport emphasizes preparation and execution (e.g., gymnastics), organize practices that focus on appropriate behaviors associated with these aspects of performance. Observe your athletes to identify specific behaviors that either benefit or hurt their preparation and execution.

☐ Identify the most effective role you can play for your athletes. Highly skilled athletes tend to have collaborative relationships with their coaches while retaining a high degree of control over much of their practice. Less skilled athletes will need more structure and guidance from their coach.

☐ Use an appropriate amount of specifically targeted feedback. Help your athletes learn to use their own sensory information to evaluate their performances by withholding feedback on a good proportion of their practice attempts. When you do provide feedback, be certain that it is tailored specifically to the athlete's skill training goal and that it is consistent with the way you are measuring progress toward that goal.

☐ For skilled athletes who know how to correct their errors but may not be able to reliably detect them, give feedback that describes what they did or what the outcome was for a particular practice attempt. For less skilled athletes, you should also provide an explanation of how to fix the problem.

☐ Take advantage of a range of practice techniques to challenge your athletes in ways that will benefit their competitive performance. Remember that performance during practice does not always translate directly to competition. Sometimes poor practice performance means that an athlete is simply being challenged and will ultimately perform quite well in competition.

Human Performance Consultant (Human Factors, Ergonomics, Usability, Skill Acquisition Specialist)

☐ Work closely with your clients to identify the issues that need to be addressed in a given project. Recognize that the focus of your work depends on the nature of the client's needs. You might be asked to identify how a person will perform in a given situation, with a certain piece of equipment, or after a certain level of training. You might be asked to evaluate how the design of a product (e.g., a car's instrument panel, a Web browser, or a pair of garden shears) influences the way a person uses it. You might be asked to determine the cause of an accident or the source of a frequently occurring injury. You might be asked to identify the best way to train people to perform a certain skill.

☐ Observe current performance behaviors to identify both the positive and negative aspects that exist. Recognize and document the interactions between the performer, the task, and the performance setting that might explain these performance behaviors.

☐ When addressing a training issue, consider the capabilities and limitations of the learners as well as the skills they need to possess and the settings they will be asked to perform in. This will help you identify the best training approaches.

☐ When evaluating a product, consider how any existing performance problems might be most effectively corrected, by either changes in the product's design, the way users are trained, or the way the performance setting influences use (or some combination of these).

☐ Recognize how performance behaviors might change over time. If a particular movement pattern is challenging, it is possible that performance quality will suffer over time as a person becomes physically or mentally fatigued. Identify ways that task demands might be made more flexible while still achieving the desired performance goals.

☐ Recognize how product uses might change over time (e.g., a screwdriver gets used as a pry bar) and help your client identify ways to ensure that alternative uses don't conflict with the tasks the product was originally designed to accomplish.

Physical or Occupational Therapist

☐ Design and use rehabilitation activities that are based on principles of motor behavior.

☐ Document how variations in your patients' behavior affect their performance of specific skills. Identify which behaviors are supportive and which are problematic with respect to the patient's rehabilitation goals. Poor functional performance can be due to pain, weakness, restricted range of motion, or a previously learned pattern of movement that is ineffective.

☐ Recognize that some patients might benefit from a more collaborative relationship (e.g., an expert athlete recovering from a recurring injury). Other patients will benefit from more frequent and specific direction (e.g., a traumatic brain injury patient during initial rehabilitation sessions).

☐ Recognize when assistive devices are appropriate to meet short-term rehabilitation goals (e.g., the use of crutches after knee surgery) and plan ways to eventually transition the patient to greater independence. Also recognize when assistive devices will be a part of a long-term solution (e.g., the use of a cane by an older person who has impaired balance) and devote a portion of time to instructing the patient in the correct use of the device.

☐ Identify and use the appropriate types of feedback during rehabilitation activities. Provide an appropriate amount of external feedback to ensure that patients learn to use the sensory information that is directly available to them as a result of their movements. Help them learn to connect this sensory information (e.g., how the movement felt) to their intended movement goals and the actual movement outcomes.

☐ Use a variety of practice techniques to take advantage of the different ways people learn. Challenge them to improve movement skills that are relevant to their functional performance in everyday life. Help your patients recognize that therapy is sometimes more (or less) challenging than real-world settings and that their performance during rehabilitation will not always indicate how they will perform once they are on their own.

☐ Be certain that rehabilitation activities match patients' goals in terms of the activities they complete, the way their performance is measured, and the feedback they receive.

☐ When it is appropriate, allow your patients to have some control over their rehabilitation experiences. This will help prepare them to continue their rehabilitation activities on their own once the clinical course of therapy is finished.

Fitness Professional

☐ Incorporate skill instruction related to exercise technique into your training sessions with clients. Correct technique maximizes training adaptations and reduces the risk of injury.

☐ Be aware that a lack of motor skills might be a barrier to exercise for some of your more sedentary clients. Even seemingly simple skills that most active people take for granted can be quite challenging for others who do not have similar movement experiences.

☐ Recognize that even fit and experienced clients may be uncomfortable demonstrating new movement skills in a public setting. For example, a client might be resistant to a group exercise class because he or she is self-conscious about making mistakes in front of others.

☐ Adopt the attitude of a teacher so that you help your clients learn to perform exercise skills correctly on their own.

☐ Observe your clients' exercise behaviors and carefully document how these behaviors affect their exercise performance. Identify which behaviors are supportive and which are problematic with respect to their fitness goals.

☐ Recognize that some clients will want a more collaborative relationship (e.g., an expert athlete) while others will want more frequent and specific direction (e.g., a new exerciser).

☐ Use a variety of practice techniques to take advantage of the different ways people learn exercise skills. Remember to teach your clients exercise skills that will benefit their fitness as it relates to their real-world activities. For example, developing skill in completing an isolation exercise (e.g., a preacher curl) might not be the most effective course of instruction for a client wanting general fitness to improve function in everyday activities that require more complex combinations of muscle activity.

☐ Identify and use the appropriate types of feedback during exercise skill instruction. Provide an appropriate amount of external feedback to ensure that your clients learn to use the sensory information that is directly available to them as a result of their movements. Help them learn to connect this sensory information (e.g., how the movement felt) to their intended movement goals and the actual movement outcomes. Self-monitoring of correct exercise form is an important skill that will allow your clients to exercise effectively and safely.

References

Adams, J.A. (1971). A closed-loop theory of motor learning. *Journal of Motor Behavior, 3,* 2, 111-149.

Adams, J.A. (1978). Theoretical issues for knowledge of results. In G.E. Stelmach (Ed.), *Information Processing in Motor Control and Learning* (pp. 229-240). New York: Academic Press.

Adams, J.A. (1987). Historical review and appraisal of research on the learning, retention, and transfer of human motor skills. *Psychological Bulletin, 101,* 41-74.

Alexander, S. (2009). 25 things you don't know about Pat Summitt. *Knoxville News Sentinel.* Retrieved June 7, 2009, from www.knoxnews.com/news/2009/jun/07/25-things-pat-summitt/.

American Occupational Therapy Association. (2007). *FAQs about OT Education.* Retrieved July 18, 2008, from www.aota.org/Students/Prospective/FAQs/38216.aspx.

Ashcroft, B. (2005). *We Wanted Wings: A History of the Aviation Cadet Program.* Retrieved January 6, 2009, from www.scribd.com/doc/1446022/US-Air-Force-AFD061109026.

Bernstein, N. (1967). *The Co-ordination and Regulation of Movements.* London: Pergamon Press.

Bloom, G.A., Crumpton, R., & Anderson, J.E. (1999). A systematic observation study of the teaching behaviors of an expert basketball coach. *Sport Psychologist, 13,* 157-170.

Bohannon, R.W., Larkin, P.A., Cook, A.C., Gear, J., & Singer, J. (1984). Decrease in timed balance test scores with aging. *Physical Therapy, 64,* 7, 1067-1070.

Bryan, W.L., & Harter, N. (1897). Studies on the telegraphic language: The acquisition of a hierarchy of habits. *Psychological Review, 6,* 345-375.

Bureau of Labor Statistics, U.S. Department of Labor. (2007). *Occupational Outlook Handbook, 2008-09 Edition.* Retrieved July 18, 2008, from www.bls.gov/oco/ocos078.htm.

Capra, F. (2007). *The Science of Leonardo.* New York: Doubleday.

Chase, W.G., & Simon, H.A. (1973). The mind's eye in chess. In W.G. Chase (Ed.), *Visual Information Processing* (pp. 404-427). New York: Academic Press.

Christina, R.W., & Corcos, D.M. (1988). *Coaches Guide to Teaching Sport Skills.* Champaign, IL: Human Kinetics.

Clegg, B. (2007). *The Man Who Stopped Time: The Illuminating Story of Eadweard Muybridge—Father of the Motion Picture, Pioneer of Photography, Murderer.* Washington, D.C.: Joseph Henry Press.

Côté, J. (1999). The influence of the family in the development of talent in sport. *The Sport Psychologist, 13,* 395-417.

Deci, E.L., & Ryan, R.M. (1985). *Intrinsic Motivation and Self-Determination in Human Behavior.* New York: Plenum Press.

Delbarre, E.B. (1894). Psychological literature: The muscular sense. *Psychological Review, 1,* 1, 100.

Draganski, B., Gaser, C., Busch, V., Schuierer, G., Bognahn, U., & May, A. (2004). Neuroplasticity: Changes in grey matter induced by training. *Nature, 427,* 311-312.

Ericsson, K.A., Krampe, R.T., & Tesch-Römer, C. (1993). The role of deliberate practice in the acquisition of expert performance. *Psychological Review, 100,* 3, 363-406.

Fairbrother, J.T. (2007a). Prediction of 1500-m freestyle swimming times for older masters All-American swimmers. *Experimental Aging Research, 33,* 3, 461-471.

Fairbrother, J.T. (2007b). Age-related changes in top ten men's US masters 50-m freestyle swim times as a function of finishing place. *Perceptual and Motor Skills, 105,* 1289-1293.

Fairbrother, J.T., & Boxell, R.L. (2008). The use of naturalistic observation to assess movement patterns and timing structure of the take-off maneuver in surfing. *Journal of Behavioral Analysis in Health, Sports, Fitness and Medicine, 1,* 1, 12-18.

Fairbrother, J.T., Hall, K.G., & Shea, J.B. (2002). Differential transfer and retention benefits in movement time and relative timing for blocked and random practice of speeded-response tasks belonging to a single movement class. *Journal of Human Movement Studies, 42,* 291-303.

Fairbrother, J.T., Readdick, C.A., & Shea, J.B. (2008). A forensic investigation of a portable crib collapse. *Ergonomics in Design, 16,* 1, 14-18.

Fairbrother, J.T., Shea, J.B., & Marzilli, T.S. (2007). Repeated retention testing effects do not generalize to a contextual interference protocol. *Research Quarterly for Exercise and Sport, 78,* 5, 465-475.

Farrow, D., & Abernethy, B. (2002). Can anticipatory skills be learned through implicit video-based perceptual training? *Journal of Sport Sciences, 20,* 6, 471-485.

Feltz, D.L., & Landers, D.M. (1983). The effects of mental practice on motor skill learning and performance: A meta-analysis. *Journal of Sport Psychology, 5,* 1, 25-57.

Fitts, P.M. (1954). The information capacity of the human motor system in controlling the amplitude of movement. *Journal of Experimental Psychology: General, 121,* 3, 262-269.

Fleishman, E.A. (1964). *The Structure and Measurement of Physical Fitness.* Englewood Cliffs, NJ: Prentice-Hall.

Frances, A. (2006). WakeWorld Rider Link. February 2006—Daniel Walden. Retrieved June 8, 2009, from www.wakeworld.com/getarticle.asp?articleid=548.

Giuffrida, C.G., Shea, J.B., & Fairbrother, J.T. (2002). Differential transfer benefits of increased practice for constant, blocked, and serial practice schedules. *Journal of Motor Behavior, 34,* 353-365.

Guadagnoli, M.A., & Lee, T.D. (2004). Challenge point: A framework for conceptualizing the effects of various practice conditions in motor learning. *Journal of Motor Behavior, 36,* 2, 212-224.

Hanin, Y.L. (2000). Individual zones of optimal functioning (IZOF) model: Emotion-performance relationships in sport. In Y.L. Hanin (Ed.), *Emotion in Sport.* Champaign, IL: Human Kinetics.

Hanlon, R.E. (1996). Motor learning following unilateral stroke. *Archives of Physical Medicine and Rehabilitation, 77,* 8, 811-815.

Harrington, J. (1984). Assessing philosophies of treatment. In E.M. Andamo (Ed.), *Guide to Program Evaluation for Physical Therapy and Occupational Therapy Services* (pp. 77-96). New York: Haworth Press.

Hendrickson, G., & Schroeder, W.H. (1941). Transfer of training in learning to hit a submerged target. *Journal of Educational Psychology, 32,* 205-213.

Henry, F.M., & Rogers, D.E. (1960). Increased response latency for complicated movements and a "memory drum" theory of neuromotor reaction. *Research Quarterly, 31,* 3, 448-458.

Hick, W.E. (1952). On the rate of gain of information. *Quarterly Journal of Experimental Psychology, 4,* 1, 11-26.

Howe, M.J.A., Davidson, J.W., & Sloboda, J.A. (1998). Innate talents: Reality or myth? *Behavioral and Brain Sciences, 21,* 399-442.

Hyman, R. (1953). Stimulus information as a determinant of reaction time. *Journal of Experimental Psychology, 45,* 3, 188-196.

Keetch, K.M., Schmidt, R.A., Lee, T.D., & Young, D.E. (2005). Especial skills: Their emergence with massive amounts of practice. *Journal of Experimental Psychology: Human Perception and Performance, 31,* 5, 970.

Kerr, R., & Booth, B. (1978). Specific and varied practice of motor skill. *Perceptual and Motor Skills, 46,* 2, 395-401.

Lee, L., & Bleecker, T. (1989). *The Bruce Lee Story.* Burbank, CA: Ohara Publications.

Lee, T.D., & Genovese, E.D. (1988). Distribution of practice in motor skill acquisition: Learning and performance effects reconsidered. *Research Quarterly for Exercise and Sport, 59,* 4, 277-287.

Lee, T.D., Ishikura, T., Kegel, S., Gonzalez, D., & Passmore, S. (2008). Head–putter coordination patterns in expert and less skilled golfers. *Journal of Motor Behavior, 40,* 4, 267-272.

Lee, T.D., & Magill, R.A. (1983). The locus of contextual interference in motor-skill acquisition. *Journal of Experimental Psychology: Learning, Memory, and Cognition, 9,* 4, 730-746.

Lee, T.D., & Magill, R.A. (1985). Can forgetting facilitate skill acquisition? In D. Goodman, R.B. Wilberg, & I.M. Franks (Eds.), *Differing Perspectives in Motor Learning, Memory, and Control* (pp. 3-22). Amsterdam: North-Holland.

Locke, E.A., & Latham, G.P. (1985). The application of goal setting to sports. *Journal of Sport Psychology, 7,* 3, 205-222.

Magill, R.A. (1998). Knowledge is more than we can talk about: Implicit learning in motor skill acquisition. *Research Quarterly for Exercise and Sport, 69,* 2, 104-110.

Magill, R.A. (2007). *Motor Learning and Control: Concepts and Applications, Eighth Edition.* New York: McGraw-Hill.

McCullagh, P. (1986). Model status as a determinant of observational learning and performance. *Journal of Sport Psychology, 8,* 319-331.

McCullagh, P. (1987). Model similarity effects on motor performance. *Journal of Sport Psychology, 9,* 249-260.

McPherson, S.L. (1999). Tactical differences in problem representations and solutions in collegiate varsity and beginner female tennis players. *Research Quarterly for Exercise and Sport, 70,* 4, 369-384.

McPherson, S.L., & Kernodle, M. (2007). Mapping two new points on the tennis expertise continuum: Tactical skills of adult advanced beginners and entry-level professionals during competition. *Journal of Sport Sciences, 25,* 8, 945-959.

Muybridge, E. (1887). *Animal Locomotion: An Electrophotographic Investigation of Consecutive Phases of Animal Movements.* Philadelphia: Lippincott.

Nideffer, R.M. (1976). *The Inner Athlete: Mind Plus Muscle for Winning.* New York: Crowell.

PE Central. (2007). Becoming a Physical Education Teacher. Retrieved July 18, 2008, from www.pecentral.org/professional/becomingapeteacher.html.

Pavlova, M., Krägeloh-Mann, I., Sokolov, A., & Birbaumer, N. (2001). Recognition of point-light biological motion displays by young children. *Perception, 30,* 8, 925-933.

PGA of America. (2008). PGA PGM Course Descriptions. Retrieved May 20, 2009, from http://pgajobfinder.pgalinks.com/helpwanted/empcenter/pgaandyou/pro.cfm?ctc=1647#SCoT.

Poulton, E.C. (1954). On prediction in skilled movements. *Psychological Bulletin, 6,* 467-478.

Prezuhy, A.M., & Etnier, J.L. (2001). Attentional patterns of horseshoe pitchers at two levels of task difficulty. *Research Quarterly for Exercise and Sport, 72,* 3, 293-298.

Proctor, R.W., & Dutta, A. (1995). *Skill Acquisition and Human Performance.* Thousand Oaks, CA: Sage.

Proctor, R.W., & Vu, K-P.L. (2006). *Stimulus-Response Compatibility Principles.* Boca Raton, FL: CRC/Taylor & Francis.

Proteau, L., Marteniuk, R.G., & Lèvesque, L. (1992). A sensorimotor basis for motor learning: Evidence indicating specificity of practice. *Quarterly Journal of Experimental Psychology Section A: Human Experimental Psychology, 44,* 3, 557-575.

Reason, J.T. (1990). *Human Error.* New York: Cambridge University Press.

Rizolatti, G., & Craighero, L. (2004). The mirror-neuron system. *Annual Review of Neuroscience, 27,* 169-192.

Saunders, F. (2008). The language playing field. *American Scientist, 96,* 6, 462. Retrieved July 8, 2009, from www.americanscientist.org/issues/pub/the-language-playing-field.

Schmidt, R.A. (1975). A schema theory of discrete motor skill learning. *Psychological Review, 82,* 4, 225-260.

Schmidt, R.A., Lange, C.A., & Young, D.E. (1990). Optimizing summary knowledge of results for skill learning. *Human Movement Science, 9,* 325-348.

Schmidt, R.A., & Lee, T.D. (2005). *Motor Control and Learning: A Behavioral Emphasis, Fourth Edition.* Champaign, IL: Human Kinetics.

Schmidt, R.A., & Sherwood, D.E. (1982). An inverted-U relation between spatial error and force requirements in rapid limb movements: Further evidence for the impulse-variability model. *Journal of Experimental Psychology: Human Perception and Performance, 8,* 1, 158-170.

Schmidt, R.A., & Wrisberg, C.A. (2008). *Motor Learning and Performance: A Situation-Based Learning Approach, Fourth Edition*. Champaign, IL: Human Kinetics.

Schmidt, R.A., Zelaznik, H., Hawkins, B., Frank, J.S., & Quinn, J.T.J. (1979). Motor output variability: A theory for the accuracy of rapid motor acts. *Psychological Review, 47*, 415-451.

Shea, J.B., & Morgan, R.L. (1979). Contextual interference effects on the acquisition, retention, and transfer of a motor skill. *Journal of Experimental Psychology: Human Learning and Memory, 5,* 2, 179-187.

Shea, J.B., & Zimny, S.T. (1983). Context effects in memory and learning movement information. In R.A. Magill (Ed.), *Memory and Control of Action* (pp. 345-366). Amsterdam: North-Holland.

Shea, J.B., & Zimny, S.T. (1988). Knowledge incorporation in motor representation. In O.G. Meijer & K. Roth (Eds.), *Complex Movement Behaviour: The Motor-Action Controversy* (pp. 289-314). Amsterdam: North-Holland.

Silva, J.M. III, & Applebaum, M.I. (1989). Association-dissociation patterns of United States Olympic marathon trial contestants. *Cognitive Therapy and Research, 13,* 2, 185-192.

Sports Hollywood. (2007). The 1954 Milan Indians: The Real "Hoosiers." Retrieved July 6, 2009, from www.sportshollywood.com/hoosiers.html.

SportSouth. February 3, 2009. Spotlight: Pat Summit. Interview with Courtney Jones. [Television documentary]. www.youtube.com/watch?v=RxOnRaSVg0A.

Stanton, N. (1997). Product design with people in mind. In N. Stanton (Ed.), *Human Factors in Consumer Products* (pp. 1-18). Boca Raton, FL: CRC Press/Taylor & Francis.

Stodden, D.F., Goodway, J.D., Langendorfer, S.J., Roberton, M.A., Rudisill, M.E., Garcia, C., & Garcia, L.E. (2008). A developmental perspective on the role of motor skill competence in physical activity: An emergent relationship. *Quest, 60,* 2, 290-306.

Swinnen, S.P., Schmidt, R.A., Nicholson, D.E., & Shapiro, D.C. (1990). Information feedback for skill acquisition: Instantaneous knowledge of results degrades learning. *Journal of Experimental Psychology: Human Learning, Memory, and Cognition, 16,* 706-716.

Upton, J. (2008, June). In hunt for Olympic gold, techies are major players. *USA Today*. Retrieved July 5, 2008, from www.usatoday.com/sports/olympics/2008-06-22-techies_N.htm.

UT Ladyvols.com. (n.d.) Basketball. Pat Summitt. Retrieved July 6, 2009, from www.utladyvols.com/sports/w-baskbl/mtt/summitt_pat00.html.

Vickers, J.N. (2007). *Perception, Cognition, and Decision Training: The Quiet Eye in Action*. Champaign, IL: Human Kinetics.

Wells, M.K. (1997). *Courage and Air Warfare: The Allied Aircrew Experience in the Second World War.* Cass series—studies in air power, 2. London, England: F. Cass.

Weinberg, R.S., & Hunt, V.V. (1976). The interrelationships between anxiety, motor performance, and electromyography. *Journal of Motor Behavior, 8,* 219-224.

Weltman, G., & Egstrom, G.H. (1966). Perceptual narrowing in novice divers. *Human Factors, 8,* 6, 499-506.

Whitall, J., Waller, S.M., Silver, K.H.C., & Macko, R.F. (2000). Repetitive bilateral arm training with rhythmic auditory cueing improves motor function in chronic hemiparetic stroke. *Stroke, 31,* 10, 2390-2395.

Williams, A. M. (2000). Perceptual skill in soccer: Implications for talent identification and development. *Journal of Sports Sciences, 18*, 737-750.

Williams, A.M., & Davids, K. (1998). Visual search strategy, selective attention, and expertise in soccer. *Research Quarterly for Exercise and Sport, 69,* 2, 111-128.

Williams, A.M., Ward, P., Knowles, J.M., & Smeeton, N.J. (2002). Anticipation skill in a real-world task: Measurement, training, and transfer in tennis. *Journal of Experimental Psychology: Applied, 8,* 4, 259-270.

Williams, A.M., Ward, P., Smeeton, N.J., & Allen, D. (2004). Developing anticipation skills in tennis using on-court instruction: Perception versus perception and action. *Journal of Applied Sport Psychology, 16,* 4, 350-360.

Winstein, C.J., & Schmidt, R.A. (1990). Reduced frequency of knowledge of results enhances motor skill learning. *Journal of Experimental Psychology: Learning, Memory, and Cognition, 16,* 4, 677-691.

Wolf, S.L., Winstein, C.J., Miller, P., Taub, E., Uswatte, G., Morris, D., Giuliani, C., Light, K., & Nichols-Larsen, D. (2006). Effect of constraint-induced movement therapy on upper extremity function 3 to 9 months after stroke: The EXCITE randomized clinical trial. *Journal of the American Medical Association, 296,* 2095-2104.

Wooden, J. (1997). *Wooden: A Lifetime of Observations and Reflections On and Off the Court.* Lincolnwood, IL: Contemporary Books.

Wooden, J.R., & Nater, S. (1996). *John Wooden's UCLA Offense.* Champaign, IL: Human Kinetics.

Woodworth, R.S. (1899). The accuracy of voluntary movement. *Psychological Review, 3,* 1-114.

Wrisberg, C.A. (1994). The arousal-performance relationship. *Quest, 46,* 1, 60-77.

Wrisberg, C.A. (2007). S*port Skill Instruction for Coaches.* Champaign, IL: Human Kinetics.

Wulf, G. (2007a). *Attention and Motor Skill Learning.* Champaign, IL: Human Kinetics.

Wulf, G. (2007b). Self-controlled practice enhances motor learning: Implications for physiotherapy. *Physiotherapy, 93,* 96-101.

Wulf, G., McConnel, N., Gartner, M., & Schwarz, A. (2002). Enhancing the learning of sport skills through external-focus feedback. *Journal of Motor Behavior, 34,* 2, 171-182.

Yerkes, R.M., & Dodson, J.D. (1908). The relation of strength of stimulus to rapidity of habit-formation. *Journal of Comparative Neurology and Psychology, 18,* 459-482.

Bibliography

Ainsworth, J., & Fox, C. (1989). Learning to learn: A cognitive processes approach to movement skills acquisition. *Strategies, 3,* 1, 20-22.

Ames, C. (1992). Achievement goals, motivational climate, and motivational processes. In G.C. Roberts (Ed.), *Motivation in Sport and Exercise* (pp. 161-176). Champaign, IL: Human Kinetics.

Anderson, D.I., Magill, R.A., & Sekiya, H. (1994). A reconsideration of the trials-delay of knowledge of results paradigm in motor skill learning. *Research Quarterly for Exercise and Sport, 65,* 3, 286-290.

Anderson, D.I., Magill, R.A., Sekiya, H., & Ryan, G. (2005). Support for an explanation of the guidance effect in motor skill learning. *Journal of Motor Behavior, 37,* 3, 231-238.

Arent, S.M., & Landers, D.M. (2003). Arousal, anxiety, and performance: A reexamination of the inverted-U hypothesis. *Research Quarterly for Exercise and Sport, 74,* 4, 436-444.

Arps, G.F. (1920). Work with knowledge of results versus work without knowledge of results. *Psychological Monographs, 28,* 1-41.

Australian Institute of Sport. (2009). Dr. Damian Farrow. Retrieved July 6, 2009, from http://ausport.gov.au/ais/sssm/psych_new/about_us/our_team/dr_damian_farrow.

Baddeley, A.D., & Longman, D.J.A. (1978). The influence of length and frequency of training session on the rate of learning to type. *Ergonomics, 21,* 8, 627-635.

Badets, A., & Blandin, Y. (2005). Observational learning: Effects of bandwidth knowledge of results. *Journal of Motor Behavior, 37,* 3, 211-216.

Bahill, A.T., & Laritz, T. (1984). Why can't batters keep their eyes on the ball? *American Scientist, 72,* 3, 249-253.

Baker, J., Côté, J., & Abernethy, B. (2003). Learning from the experts: Practice activities of expert decision makers in sport. *Research Quarterly for Exercise and Sport, 74,* 3, 342-347.

Baker, J., Côté, J., & Abernethy, B. (2003). Sport-specific practice and the development of expert decision-making in team ball sports. *Journal of Applied Sport Psychology, 15,* 1, 12-25.

Barrett, D.D., & Burton, A.W. (2002). Throwing patterns used by collegiate baseball players in actual games. *Research Quarterly for Exercise and Sport, 73,* 1, 19-27.

Bartlett, F.C. (1995). *Remembering: A Study in Experimental and Social Psychology.* Cambridge: Cambridge University Press.

Battig, W.F. (1966). Facilitation and interference. In E.A. Bilodeau (Ed.), *Acquisition of Skill* (pp. 215-244). New York: Academic Press.

Beek, P.J., & Van Santvoord, A.A.M. (1992). Learning the cascade juggle: A dynamical systems analysis. *Journal of Motor Behavior, 24,* 1, 85-94.

Behrman, A.L., Teitelbaum, P., & Cauraugh, J.H. (1998). Verbal instructional sets to normalize the temporal and spatial gait variables in Parkinson's disease. *British Medical Journal, 65,* 580-582.

Beilock, S.L., & Carr, T.H. (2001). On the fragility of skilled performance: What governs choking under pressure? *Journal of Experimental Psychology: General, 130,* 4, 701-725.

Beilock, S.L., & Carr, T.H. (2004). From novice to expert performance: Memory, attention, and the control of complex sensorimotor skills. In A.M. Williams & N.J. Hodges (Eds.), *Skill Acquisition in Sport: Research, Theory and Practice* (pp. 309-327). London: Routledge.

Bilodeau, E.A., Bilodeau, I.M., & Schumsky, D.A. (1959). Some effects of introducing and withdrawing knowledge of results early and late in practice. *Journal of Experimental Psychology, 58,* 142-144.

Blandin, Y., Lhuisset, L., & Proteau, L. (1999). Cognitive processes underlying observational learning of motor skills. *Quarterly Journal of Experimental Psychology Section A, 52,* 4, 957-979.

Blandin, Y., & Proteau, L. (2000). On the cognitive basis of observational learning: Development of mechanisms for the detection and correction of errors. *Quarterly Journal of Experimental Psychology Section A, 53,* 3, 846-867.

Boschker, M.S.J., Bakker, F.C., & Michaels, C.F. (2002). Memory for the functional characteristics of climbing walls: Perceiving affordances. *Journal of Motor Behavior, 34,* 1, 25-36.

Bowditch, H.P., & Southard, W.F. (1882). A comparison of sight and touch. *Journal of Physiology, 3,* 232-254.

Boyce, B.A., & Del Rey, P. (1990). Designing applied research in a naturalistic setting using a contextual interference paradigm. *Journal of Human Movement Studies, 18,* 189-200.

Bransford, J.D., Franks, J.J., Morris, C.D., & Stein, B.S. (1979). Some general constraints on learning and memory research. In L.S. Cermak & F.I.M. Craik (Eds.), *Levels of Processing in Human Memory* (pp. 331-354). Hillsdale, NJ: Erlbaum.

Bryan, W.L., & Harter, N. (1899). Studies in the physiology and psychology of the telegraphic language. *Psychological Review, 4,* 27-53.

Bund, A., & Wiemeyer, J. (2004). Self-controlled learning of a complex motor skill: Effects of the learners' preferences on performance and self-efficacy. *Journal of Human Movement Studies, 47,* 215-236.

Button, C., Macleod, M., Sanders, R., & Coleman, S. (2003). Examining movement variability in the basketball free-throw action at different skill levels. *Research Quarterly for Exercise and Sport, 74,* 3, 257-269.

Catalano, J.F., & Kleiner, B.M. (1984). Distant transfer in coincident timing as a function of variability of practice. *Perceptual and Motor Skills, 58,* 3, 851-856.

Chambers, K.L., & Vickers, J.N. (2006). Effects of bandwidth feedback and questioning on the performance of competitive swimmers. *Sport Psychologist, 20,* 2, 184.

Chiviacowsky, S., & Wulf, G. (2002). Self-controlled feedback: Does it enhance learning because performers get feedback when they need it? *Research Quarterly for Exercise and Sport, 73,* 4, 408-415.

Chiviacowsky, S., & Wulf, G. (2005). Self-controlled feedback is effective if it is based on the learner's performance. *Research Quarterly for Exercise and Sport, 76,* 1, 42-48.

Chiviacowsky, S., & Wulf, G. (2007). Feedback after good trials enhances learning. *Research Quarterly for Exercise and Sport, 78,* 1, 40-47.

Christina, R.W., Barresi, J.V., & Shaffner, P. (1990). The development of response selection accuracy in a football linebacker using video training. *Sport Psychologist, 4,* 11-17.

Christina, R.W., & Shea, J.B. (1993). More on assessing the retention of motor learning based on restricted information. *Research Quarterly for Exercise and Sport, 64,* 2, 217-222.

Clark, S.E. (2007). The impact of self-as-a-model interventions on children's self-regulation of learning and swimming performance. *Journal of Sports Sciences, 25,* 5, 577-586.

Cochran, M. (1930). Kinesthesis and the piano. *Australian Journal of Psychology, 8,* 205-209.

Corbetta, D., & Bojczyk, K.E. (2002). Infants return to two-handed reaching when they are learning to walk. *Journal of Motor Behavior, 34,* 1, 83-95.

Corbetta, D., & Thelen, E. (1996). The developmental origins of bimanual coordination: A dynamic perspective. *Journal of Experimental Psychology: Human Perception and Performance, 22,* 502-522.

Corbetta, D., Thelen, E., & Johnson, K. (2000). Motor constraints on the development of perception-action matching in infant reaching. *Infant Behavior and Development, 23,* 351-374.

Crossman, E. (1959). A theory of the acquisition of speed skill. *Ergonomics, 2,* 2, 153-166.

Cuddy, L.J., & Jacoby, L.L. (1982). When forgetting helps memory: An analysis of repetition effects. *Journal of Verbal Learning and Verbal Behavior, 21,* 4, 451-467.

Dempster, F.N. (1988). The spacing effect. *American Psychologist, 43,* 627-634.

Drowatzky, J.N., & Zuccato, F.C. (1967). Interrelationships between selected measures of static and dynamic balance. *Research Quarterly, 38,* 3, 509-510.

Druckman, D., & Bjork, R.A. (1991). *In the Mind's Eye: Enhancing Human Performance.* Washington, D.C.: National Academy Press.

Easterbrook, J.A. (1959). The effect of emotion on cue utilization and the organization of behavior. *Psychological Review, 66,* 3, 183-201.

Elliott, D., Helsen, W.F., & Chua, R. (2001). A century later: Woodworth's (1899) two-component model of goal-directed aiming. *Psychological Bulletin, 127,* 3, 342-357.

Elwell, J.L., & Grindley, G.C. (1938). The effect of knowledge of results on learning and performance. *British Journal of Psychology, 29,* 39-54.

Ericsson, K.A. (1996). The acquisition of expert performance: An introduction to some of the issues. In K.A. Ericsson (Ed.), *The Road to Excellence: The Acquisition of Expert Performance in the Arts and Sciences, Sports, and Games* (pp. 1-50). Mahwah, NJ: Erlbaum.

Espenchade, A. (1940). Motor performance in adolescence, including the study of relationships with measures of physical growth and maturity. *Monographs of the Society for Research in Child Development, 5* (serial no. 24).

Fairbrother, J.T. (2008). *Instructor Guide for "Practical Laboratory Activities."* Champaign, IL: Human Kinetics. Ancillary for Schmidt, R.A. & Wrisberg, C.A. (2008), *Motor Learning and Performance, Fourth Edition.* Champaign, IL: Human Kinetics.

Fairbrother, J.T. (2008). *Practical Laboratory Activities.* Champaign, IL: Human Kinetics. Ancillary for Schmidt, R.A. & Wrisberg, C.A. (2008), *Motor Learning and Performance, Fourth Edition.* Champaign, IL: Human Kinetics.

Fairbrother, J.T., & Brueckner, S. (2008). Task switching effects in anticipation timing. *Research Quarterly for Exercise and Sport, 79,* 1, 116-121.

Fairbrother, J.T., Brueckner, S., & Barros, J.A.C. (2009). The effects of switching between targets on the performance of a simple motor skill. *Human Movement Science, 28,* 1-11.

Fairbrother, J.T., & Shea, J.B. (2005). The effects of a single reminder trial on the retention of a motor skill. *Research Quarterly for Exercise and Sport, 76,* 1, 49-59.

Farrow, D., Abernethy, B., & Jackson, R.C. (2005). Probing expert anticipation with the temporal occlusion paradigm: Experimental investigations of some methodological issues. *Motor Control, 9,* 3, 332-351.

Fitts, P.M., & Peterson, J.R. (1964). Information capacity of discrete motor responses. *Journal of Experimental Psychology, 67,* 2, 103-112.

Fitts, P.M., & Posner, M.I. (1967). *Human Performance.* Belmont, CA: Brooks/Cole.

Fleishman, E.A. (1956). Psychomotor selection tests: Research and application in the United States Air Force. *Personnel Psychology, 9,* 4, 449-467.

Fleishman, E.A., & Bartlett, C.J. (1969). Human abilities. *Annual Review of Psychology, 20,* 1, 349-380.

Fleishman, E.A., & Hempel Jr., W.E. (1955). The relation between abilities and improvement with practice in a visual discrimination reaction task. *Journal of Experimental Psychology, 49,* 5, 301-312.

Franz, E.A., Zelaznik, H.N., & Smith, A. (1992). Evidence of common timing processes in the control of manual, orofacial and speech movements. *Journal of Motor Behavior, 24,* 3, 281-287.

Franz, E.A., Zelaznik, H.N., Swinnen, S.S., & Walter, C. (2001). Spatial conceptual influences on the coordination of bimanual actions: When a dual task becomes a single task. *Journal of Motor Behavior, 33,* 1, 103-112.

Gabriele, T.E., Hall, C.R., & Lee, T.D. (1989). Cognition in motor learning: Imagery effects on contextual interference. *Human Movement Science, 8,* 3, 227-245.

Gentile, A.M. (1972). A working model of skill acquisition with application to teaching. *Quest, 17,* 3-23.

Gibson, J. (1966). *The Senses Considered as Perceptual Systems.* Boston: Houghton Mifflin.

Gibson, J.J. (1979). *The Ecological Approach to Perception.* Boston: Houghton Mifflin.

Goode, S., & Magill, R.A. (1986). Contextual interference effects in learning three badminton serves. *Research Quarterly for Exercise and Sport, 57,* 4, 308-314.

Gregg, M., & Hall, C. (2006). The relationship of skill level and age to the use of imagery by golfers. *Journal of Applied Sport Psychology, 18,* 4, 363-375.

Griffith, C.R. (1931). An experiment on learning to drive a golf ball. *Athletic Journal, 11,* 11-13.

Guadagnoli, M., Holcomb, W., & Davis, M. (2002). The efficacy of video feedback for learning the golf swing. *Journal of Sports Sciences, 20,* 8, 615-622.

Guadagnoli, M.A., & Kohl, R.M. (2001). Knowledge of results for motor learning: Relationship between error estimation and knowledge of results frequency. *Journal Motor Behavior, 33,* 2, 217-224.

Guthrie, E.R. (1952). *The Psychology of Learning.* New York: Harper & Row.

Hall, K.G., Domingues, D.A., & Cavazos, R. (1994). Contextual interference effects with skilled baseball players. *Perceptual and Motor Skills, 78,* 3, 835-841.

Hall, K.G., & Magill, R.A. (1995). Variability of practice and contextual interference in motor skill learning. *Journal of Motor Behavior, 27,* 299-309.

Harle, S.K., & Vickers, J.N. (2001). Training quiet eye improves accuracy in the basketball free throw. *Sport Psychologist, 15,* 3, 289-305.

Hatfield, J., & Murphy, S. (2007). The effects of mobile phone use on pedestrian crossing behaviour at signalised and unsignalised intersections. *Accident Analysis and Prevention, 39,* 1, 197-205.

Haywood, K.M. (1986). *Life Span Motor Development.* Champaign, IL: Human Kinetics.

Haywood, K.M., & Getchell, N. (2005). *Life Span Motor Development.* Champaign, IL: Human Kinetics.

Helmuth, L.L., & Ivry, R.B. (1996). When two hands are better than one: Reduced timing variability during bimanual movements. *Journal of Experimental Psychology: Human Perception and Performance, 22,* 278-293.

Henry, F.M. (1961). Reaction time-movement time correlations. *Perceptual and Motor Skills, 12,* 63-66.

Hill, L.B., Rejall, A.E., & Thorndike, E.L. (1913). Practice in the case of typewriting. *Pedagogical Seminary, 20,* 516-529.

Hogan, J.C., & Yanowitz, B.A. (1978). The role of verbal estimates of movement error in ballistic skill acquisition. *Journal of Motor Behavior, 10,* 2, 133-138.

Hollingworth, H.L. (1909). The inaccuracy of movement. *Archives of Psychology, 13,* 1-87.

Horn, R.R., Williams, A.M., Scott, M.A., & Hodges, N.J. (2005). Visual search and coordination changes in response to video and point-light demonstrations without KR. *Journal of Motor Behavior, 37,* 4, 265-274.

Hubbard, A.W., & Seng, C.N. (1954). Visual movements of batters. *Research Quarterly, 25,* 1, 42-57.

Hull, C.L. (1943). *Principles of Behavior.* New York: Appleton-Century-Crofts.

Ivry, R.B., & Hazeltine, R.E. (1995). Perception and production of temporal intervals across a range of durations: Evidence for a common timing mechanism. *Journal of Experimental Psychology: Human Perception and Performance, 21,* 1, 3-18.

Jacoby, L.L., Bjork, R.A., & Kelley, C.M. (1994). Illusions of comprehension, competence, and remembering. In D. Druckman & R.A. Bjork (Eds.), *Learning, Remembering, Believing: Enhancing Human Performance* (pp. 57-80). Washington, D.C.: National Academy Press.

Jagacinski, R.J., Greenberg, N., & Liao, M.J. (1997). Tempo, rhythm, and aging in golf. *Journal of Motor Behavior, 29,* 2, 159-173.

Jagacinski, R.J., Repperger, D.W., Moran, M.S., Ward, S.L., & Glass, B. (1980). Fitts' law and the microstructure of rapid discrete movements. *Journal of Experimental Psychology: Human Perception and Performance, 6,* 2, 309-320.

James, W. (1890). *The Principles of Psychology.* New York: Holt, Reinhart, & Winston.

Janelle, C.M., Barba, D.A., Frehlich, S.G., Tennant, L.K., & Cauraugh, J.H. (1997). Maximizing performance feedback effectiveness through videotape replay and a self-controlled learning environment. *Research Quarterly for Exercise and Sport, 68,* 4, 269-279.

Janelle, C.M., Kim, J., & Singer, R.N. (1995). Subject-controlled performance feedback and learning of a closed motor skill. *Perceptual and Motor Skills, 81,* 2, 627-634.

Janelle, C.M., Singer, R.N., & Williams, A.M. (1999). External distraction and attentional narrowing: Visual search evidence. *Journal of Sport and Exercise Psychology, 21,* 70-91.

John, D., Bassett, D.R., Thompson, D.L., Fairbrother, J.T., & Baldwin, D.R. (in press). Effect of using a treadmill workstation on performance of simulated office work tasks. *Journal of Physical Activity and Health.*

Kahneman, D. (1973). *Attention and Effort.* Englewood Cliffs, NJ: Prentice-Hall.

Kato, T., & Fukuda, T. (2002). Visual search strategies of baseball batters: Eye movements during the preparatory phase of batting. *Perceptual and Motor Skills, 94,* 2, 380-386.

Keele, S.W., & Hawkins, H.L. (1982). Explorations of individual differences relevant to high skill level. *Journal of Motor Behavior, 14,* 1, 3-23.

Keele, S.W., Ivry, R.I., & Pokorny, R.A. (1987). Force control and its relation to timing. *Journal of Motor Behavior, 19,* 1, 96-114.

Keele, S.W., Pokorny, R.A., Corcos, D.M., & Ivry, R. (1985). Do perception and motor production share common timing mechanisms: A correctional analysis. *Acta Psychologica, 60,* 173-191.

Keele, S.W., & Posner, M.I. (1968). Processing of visual feedback in rapid movements. *Journal of Experimental Psychology, 77,* 1, 155-158.

Kelso, J.A.S. (Ed.). (1995). *Dynamic Patterns: The Self-Organization of Brain and Behavior.* Cambridge, MA: MIT Press.

Kelso, J.A.S., & Clark, J.E. (1982). *The Development of Movement Control and Co-ordination.* Chichester, England: Wiley.

Kelso, J.A.S., & Schoner, G. (1988). Self-organization of coordinative movement patterns. *Human Movement Science, 7,* 1, 27-46.

Kernodle, M.W., & Carlton, L.G. (1992). Information feedback and the learning of multiple-degree-of-freedom activities. *Journal of Motor Behavior, 24,* 2, 187-196.

Klapp, S.T., Hill, M.D., Tyler, J.G., Martin, Z.E., Jagacinski, R.J., & Jones, M.R. (1985). On marching to two different drummers: Perceptual aspects of the difficulties. *Journal of Experimental Psychology: Human Perception and Performance, 11,* 6, 814-827.

Konttinen, N., Mononen, K., Viitasalo, J., & Mets, T. (2004). The effects of augmented auditory feedback on psychomotor skill learning in precision shooting. *Journal of Sport and Exercise Psychology, 26,* 2, 306-316.

Landers, D.M., Boutcher, S.H., & Wang, M.Q. (1986). A psychobiological study of archery performance. *Research Quarterly for Exercise and Sport, 57,* 236-244.

Landin, D., & Hebert, E.P. (1997). A comparison of three practice schedules along the contextual interference continuum. *Research Quarterly for Exercise and Sport, 68,* 4, 357-361.

Langfeld, H.S. (1915). Facilitation and inhibition of motor impulses: A study in simultaneous and alternating finger movements. *Psychological Review, 22,* 453-478.

Lavery, J.J. (1962). Retention of simple motor skills as a function of type of knowledge of results. *Canadian Journal of Psychology, 16,* 300-311.

Lavery, J.J., & Suddon, F.H. (1962). Retention of simple motor skills as a function of the number of trials by which KR is delayed. *Perceptual and Motor Skills, 15,* 231-237.

Lee, D.N., Lishman, J.R., & Thomson, J.A. (1982). Regulation of gait in long jumping. *Journal of Experimental Psychology, 8,* 3, 448-459.

Lee, D.N., Young, D.S., & Rewt, D. (1992). How do somersaulters land on their feet? *Journal of Experimental Psychology: Human Perception and Performance, 18,* 1195-1202.

Lee, T.D. (1998). On the dynamics of motor learning research. *Research Quarterly for Exercise and Sport, 69,* 4, 334-337.

Lee, T.D., Magill, R.A., & Weeks, D.J. (1985). Influence of practice schedule on testing schema theory predictions in adults. *Journal of Motor Behavior, 17,* 3, 283-299.

Lee, T.D., Swinnen, S.P., & Serrien, D.J. (1994). Cognitive effort and motor learning. *Quest, 46,* 328-344.

Lee, T.D., & Wishart, L.R. (2005). Motor learning conundrums (and possible solutions). *Quest, 57,* 67-78.

Lee, T.D., Wulf, G., & Schmidt, R.A. (1992). Contextual interference in motor learning: Dissociated effects due to the nature of task variations. *Quarterly Journal of Experimental Psychology Section A, 44,* 4, 627-644.

Lersten, K.C. (1968). Transfer of movement components in a motor learning task. *Research Quarterly, 39,* 3, 575-581.

Lindahl, L.G. (1945). Movement analysis as an industrial training method. *Journal of Applied Psychology, 29,* 420-436.

Liu, Y.T., Mayer-Kress, G., & Newell, K.M. (2003). Beyond curve fitting: A dynamical systems account of exponential learning in a discrete timing task. *Journal of Motor Behavior, 35,* 2, 197-207.

Lotter, W.S. (1960). Interrelationships among reaction times and speeds of movement in different limbs. *Research Quarterly, 31,* 147-155.

Mackay, D.G. (1981). The problem of rehearsal or mental practice. *Journal of Motor Behavior, 13,* 4, 274-285.

MacKenzie, I.S. (1992). Fitts' law as a research and design tool in human-computer interaction. *Human-Computer Interaction, 7,* 1, 91-139.

Magill, R.A. (2001). *Motor Learning and Control: Concepts and Applications, Seventh Edition.* New York: McGraw-Hill.

Magill, R.A., & Hall, K.G. (1990). A review of the contextual interference effect in motor skill acquisition. *Human Movement Science, 9,* 241-289.

Magill, R.A., & Wood, C.A. (1986). Knowledge of results precision as a learning variable in motor skill acquisition. *Research Quarterly for Exercise and Sport, 57,* 3, 170-173.

Magnuson, C.E., Shea, J.B., & Fairbrother, J.T. (2004). Effects of repeated retention tests on learning a single timing task. *Research Quarterly for Exercise and Sport, 75,* 39-46.

Martell, S.G., & Vickers, J.N. (2004). Gaze characteristics of elite and near-elite athletes in ice hockey defensive tactics. *Human Movement Science, 22,* 6, 689-712.

Marteniuk, R.G. (1974). Individual differences in motor performance and learning. *Exercise and Sport Sciences Reviews, 2,* 103.

Martens, R. (1987). *Coaches Guide to Sport Psychology.* Champaign, IL: Human Kinetics.

Maxwell, J.P., Masters, R.S.W., Kerr, E., & Weedon, E. (2001). The implicit benefit of learning without errors. *Quarterly Journal of Experimental Psychology Section A, 54,* 4, 1049-1068.

McCloy, C.H. (1934). The measurement of general motor capacity and general motor ability. *Research Quarterly, 5S,* 45-61.

McCullagh, P., & Little, W.S. (1989). A comparison of modalities in modeling. *Human Performance, 2,* 2, 101-111.

McCullagh, P., & Meyer, K.N. (1997). Learning versus correct models: Influence of model type on the learning of a free-weight squat lift. *Research Quarterly for Exercise and Sport, 68,* 56-61.

McLeod, P., & Dienes, Z. (1996). Do fielders know where to go to catch the ball or only how to get there? *Journal of Experimental Psychology: Human Perception and Performance, 22,* 3, 531-543.

Meijer, O.G., & Roth, K. (Eds.). (1988). *Complex Movement Behaviour: The Motor-Action Controversy.* Amsterdam: North-Holland.

Meyer, D.E., Abrams, R.A., Kornblum, S., Wright, C.E., & Smith, J.E.K. (1988). Optimality in human motor performance: Ideal control of rapid aimed movements. *Psychological Review, 95,* 3, 340-370.

Miller, G.A. (1956). The magical number seven, plus or minus two: Some limits on our capacity for processing information. *Psychological Review, 63,* 81-97.

Murphy, H.H. (1916). Distribution of practice periods in learning. *Journal of Educational Psychology, 7,* 150-162.

Nashner, L., & Berthoz, A. (1978). Visual contribution to rapid motor responses during postural control. *Brain Research, 150,* 2, 403-407.

Neumann, O. (1987). Beyond capacity: A functional view of attention. In H. Heuer & A.F. Sanders (Eds.), *Perspectives on Perception and Action* (Vol. 14, pp. 361-394). Hillsdale, NJ: Erlbaum.

Newell, K.M. (1985). Coordination, control, and skill. In D. Goodman, R.B. Wilberg, & I.M. Franks (Eds.), *Differing Perspectives in Motor Learning, Memory, and Control* (pp. 295-317). Amsterdam: North-Holland.

Newell, K.M. (1991). Motor skill acquisition. *Annual Review of Psychology, 42,* 1, 213-237.

Newell, K.M. (2003). Schema theory (1975): Retrospectives and perspectives. *Research Quarterly for Exercise and Sport, 74,* 4, 383-388.

Newell, K.M., Carlton, M.J., & Antoniou, A. (1990). The interaction of criterion and feedback information in learning a drawing task. *Journal of Motor Behavior, 22,* 4, 536-552.

Newell, K.M., Carlton, L.G., & Carlton, M.J. (1980). Velocity as a factor in movement timing accuracy. *Journal of Motor Behavior, 12,* 1, 47-56.

Orlick, T., & Partington, J. (1988). Mental links to excellence. *Sport Psychologist, 2,* 2, 105-130.

Panchuk, D., & Vickers, J.N. (2006). Gaze behaviors of goaltenders under spatial–temporal constraints. *Human Movement Science, 25,* 6, 733-752.

Pew, R.W. (1974). Levels of analysis in motor control. *Brain Research, 71,* 393-400.

Physical Therapy Clinical Research Network. (n.d.). Carolee J. Winstein, PH.D., P.T., FAPTA. Retrieved July 6, 2009, from http://pt2.usc.edu/clinresnet/bio/cwinstein.html.

Pigott, R., & Shapiro, D. (1984). Motor schema: The structure of the variability session. *Research Quarterly for Exercise and Sport, 55,* 1, 41-45.

Polit, A., & Bizzi, E. (1978). Processes controlling arm movements in monkeys. *Science, 201,* 1235-1237.

Polit, A., & Bizzi, E. (1979). Characteristics of motor programs underlying arm movements in monkeys. *Journal of Neurophysiology, 42,* 1, 183-194.

Poolton, J.M., Masters, R.S.W., & Maxwell, J.P. (2005). The relationship between initial errorless learning conditions and subsequent performance. *Human Movement Science, 24,* 3, 362-378.

Poolton, J.M., Maxwell, J.P., Masters, R.S.W., & Raab, M. (2006). Benefits of an external focus of attention: Common coding or conscious processing? *Journal of Sports Sciences, 24,* 1, 89-99.

Prinz, W. (1997). Perception and action planning. *European Journal of Cognitive Psychology, 9,* 2, 129-154.

Proteau, L., & Isabelle, G. (2002). On the role of visual afferent information for the control of aiming movements toward targets of different sizes. *Journal of Motor Behavior, 34,* 4, 367-384.

Quesada, D.C., & Schmidt, R.A. (1970). A test of the Adams-Creamer decay hypothesis for the timing of motor responses. *Journal of Motor Behavior, 2,* 273-283.

Radlo, S.J., Janelle, C.M., Barba, D.A., & Frehlich, S.G. (2001). Perceptual decision making for baseball pitch recognition: Using P300 latency and amplitude to index attentional processing. *Research Quarterly for Exercise and Sport, 72,* 1, 22-31.

Readdick, C., Shea, J.B., & Fairbrother, J.T. (2000). An investigation on the capabilities of children aged 17-24 months to self-collapse a Playskool Trav'l Lite portable crib. Submitted to Schwartz, Cooper, Greenberger and Krauss.

Roberton, M.A. (1984). Changing motor patterns during childhood. In J.R. Thomas (Ed.), *Motor Development during Childhood and Adolescence* (pp. 48-90). Minneapolis: Burgess.

Robertson, S.D., Zelaznik, H.N., Lantero, D.A., Bojczyk, K.G., Spencer, R.M., Doffin, J.G., et al. (1999). Correlations for timing consistency among tapping and drawing tasks: Evidence against a single timing process for motor control. *Journal of Experimental Psychology: Human Perception and Performance, 25,* 1316-1330.

Robin, C., Toussaint, L., Blandin, Y., & Vinter, A. (2004). Sensory integration in the learning of aiming toward "self-defined" targets. *Research Quarterly for Exercise and Sport, 75,* 4, 381-387.

Roediger, H.L., & Karpicke, J.D. (2006). The power of testing memory: Basic research and implications for educational practice. *Perspectives on Psychological Science, 1,* 3, 181-210.

Roediger, H.L., & Karpicke, J.D. (2006). Test-enhanced learning. *Psychological Science, 17,* 3, 249-255.

Rosenbaum, D.A. (1980). Human movement initiation: Specification of arm, direction, and extent. *Journal of Experimental Psychology: General, 109,* 4, 444-474.

Rosenbaum, D.A. (1991). *Human Motor Control.* San Diego: Academic Press.

Salmoni, A.W., Schmidt, R.A., & Walter, C.B. (1984). Knowledge of results and motor learning: A review and critical reappraisal. *Psychological Bulletin, 95,* 355-386.

Schmidt, R.A. (1969). Movement time as a determiner of timing accuracy. *Journal of Experimental Psychology, 79,* 1, 43-55.

Schmidt, R.A. (1985). The search for invariance in skilled movement behavior. *Research Quarterly for Exercise and Sport, 56,* 2, 188-200.

Schmidt, R.A. (2003). Motor schema theory after 27 years: Reflections and implications for a new theory. *Research Quarterly for Exercise and Sport, 74,* 4, 366-375.

Schmidt, R.A., & Bjork, R.A. (1992). New conceptualizations of practice: Common principles in three paradigms suggest new concepts for training. *Psychological Science, 3,* 4, 207-217.

Schmidt, R.A., & Gordon, G.B. (1977). Errors in motor responding, "rapid" corrections, and false anticipations. *Journal of Motor Behavior, 9,* 101-111.

Schmidt, R.A., & White, J.L. (1972). Evidence for an error detection mechanism in motor skills: A test of Adams' closed-loop theory. *Journal of Motor Behavior, 4,* 3, 143-153.

Schmidt, R.A., & Wulf, G. (1997). Continuous concurrent feedback degrades skill learning: Implications for training and simulation. *Human Factors, 39,* 4, 509-525.

Schmidt, R.A., & Young, D.E. (1987). Transfer of motor control in motor skill learning. In S.M. Cormier & J.D. Hagman (Eds.), *Transfer of Learning* (pp. 47-79). Orlando, FL: Academic Press.

Schmidt, R.A., Young, D.E., Swinnen, S., & Shapiro, D.C. (1989). Summary knowledge of results for skill acquisition: Support for the guidance hypothesis. *Journal of Experimental Psychology: Learning, Memory, and Cognition, 15,* 2, 352-359.

Schneider, D.M., & Schmidt, R.A. (1995). Units of action in motor control: Role of response complexity and target speed. *Human Performance, 8,* 1, 27-49.

Seat, J.E., & Wrisberg, C.A. (1996). The visual instruction system. *Research Quarterly for Exercise and Sport, 67,* 1, 106-108.

Shapiro, D.C., Zernicke, R.F., & Gregor, R.J. (1981). Evidence for generalized motor programs using gait pattern analysis. *Journal of Motor Behavior, 13,* 1, 33-47.

Shea, C.H., Kohl, R., & Indermill, C. (1990). Contextual interference: Contributions of practice. *Acta Psychologica, 73,* 2, 145-157.

Shea, C.H., Wright, D.L., Wulf, G., & Whitacre, C. (2000). Physical and observational practice afford unique learning opportunities. *Journal of Motor Behavior, 32,* 1, 27-36.

Shea, C.H., & Wulf, G. (2005). Schema theory: A critical appraisal and reevaluation. *Journal of Motor Behavior, 37,* 2, 85-102.

Shea, C.H., Wulf, G., Park, J.H., & Gaunt, B. (2001). Effects of an auditory model on the learning of relative and absolute timing. *Journal of Motor Behavior, 33,* 2, 127-138.

Shea, C.H., Wulf, G., Whitacre, C.A., & Park, J.H. (2001). Surfing the implicit wave. *Quarterly Journal of Experimental Psychology Section A, 54,* 3, 841-862.

Shea, J.B., & Fairbrother, J.T. (2005). Practice schedules and motor skill expertise. In W. Starosta & S. Squatrito (Eds.), *Scientific Fundamentals of Human Movement and Sport Practice* (pp. 110-117). Bologna, Italy: Centro Universitario Sportivo Bolognese.

Sherrington, C.S. (1906). *The Integrative Action of the Nervous System.* New Haven, CT: Yale University Press.

Sherwood, D.E. (1988). Effect of bandwidth knowledge of results on movement consistency. *Perceptual and Motor Skills, 66,* 2, 535-542.

Sherwood, D.E., & Lee, T.D. (2003). Schema theory: Critical review and implications for the role of cognition in a new theory of motor learning. *Research Quarterly for Exercise and Sport, 74,* 4, 376-382.

Sherwood, D.E., Schmidt, R.A., & Walter, C.B. (1988). The force/force-variability relationship under controlled temporal conditions. *Journal of Motor Behavior, 20,* 2, 106-116.

Shiffrin, R.M., & Schneider, W. (1977). Controlled and automatic human information processing: II. Perceptual learning, automatic attending, and a general theory. *Psychological Review, 84,* 2, 127-190.

Simon, D.A., & Bjork, R.A. (2001). Metacognition in motor learning. *Journal of Experimental Psychology: Learning, Memory, and Cognition, 27,* 4, 907-912.

Singer, R.N. (1968). *Motor Learning and Human Performance: An Application to Physical Education Skills.* New York: Macmillan.

Singer, R.N., Lidor, R., & Cauraugh, J.H. (1993). To be aware or not aware? What to think about while learning and performing a motor skill. *Sport Psychologist, 7,* 19-30.

Slater-Hammel, A.T. (1960). Reliability, accuracy, and refractoriness of a transit reaction. *Research Quarterly, 31,* 217-228.

Smith, P.J., Taylor, S.J., & Withers, K. (1997). Applying bandwidth feedback scheduling to a golf shot. *Research Quarterly for Exercise and Sport, 68,* 3, 215-221.

Snoddy, G.S. (1926). Learning and stability: A psychophysical analysis of a case of motor learning with clinical applications. *Journal of Applied Psychology, 10,* 1-36.

Southard, D. (1989). Changes in limb striking pattern: Effects of speed and accuracy. *Research Quarterly for Exercise and Sport, 60,* 4, 348-356.

Southard, D. (2006). Changing throwing pattern: Instruction and control parameter. *Research Quarterly for Exercise and Sport, 77,* 3, 316-325.

Southard, D., & Higgins, T. (1987). Changing movement patterns: Effects of demonstration and practice. *Research Quarterly for Exercise and Sport, 58,* 77-80.

Starkes, J.L., & Allard, F. (Eds.) (1993). *Cognitive Issues in Motor Expertise.* Amsterdam: Elsevier Science.

Stauffer, R. (2007). *The Roger Federer Story: Quest for Perfection.* New York: New Chapter Press.

Steenbergen, B., Marteniuk, R.G., & Kalbfleisch, L.E. (1995). Achieving coordination in prehension: Joint freezing and postural contributions. *Journal of Motor Behavior, 27,* 4, 333-348.

Ste-Marie, D.M., Clark, S.E., Findlay, L.C., & Latimer, A.E. (2004). High levels of contextual interference enhance handwriting skill acquisition. *Journal of Motor Behavior, 36,* 3, 115-126.

Sternad, D. (1998). A dynamic systems perspective to perception and action. *Research Quarterly for Exercise and Sport, 69,* 4, 319-325.

Sternad, D., Duarte, M., Katsumata, H., & Schaal, S. (2001). Bouncing a ball: Tuning into dynamic stability. *Journal of Experimental Psychology: Human Perception and Performance, 27,* 5, 1163-1184.

Stimpel, E. (1933). Der Wurk [The throw]. *Neue Psychologische Studien, 9,* 105-138.

Stroop, J.R. (1935). Studies of interference in serial verbal reactions. *Journal of Experimental Psychology, 18,* 6, 643-662.

Summers, J.J. (1975). The role of timing in motor program representation. *Journal of Motor Behavior, 7,* 4, 229-241.

Taub, E., & Berman, A.J. (1968). Movement and learning in the absence of sensory feedback. In S.J. Freedman (Ed.), *The Neuropsychology of Spatially Oriented Behavior* (pp. 173-192). Homewood, IL: Dorsey Press.

Thain, E. (2002). *Science and Golf IV.* London: Routledge.

Thomas, J.R. (1997). Motor behavior. In J.D. Massengale & R.A. Swanson (Eds.), *The History of Exercise and Sport Science.* Champaign, IL: Human Kinetics.

Thorndike, E.L. (1909). A note on the accuracy of discrimination of weights and lengths. *Psychological Review, 16,* 5, 340-346.

Thorndike, E.L. (1927). The law of effect. *American Journal of Psychology, 39,* 212-222.

Tremblay, L., & Proteau, L. (2001). Specificity of practice in a ball interception task. *Canadian Journal of Experimental Psychology, 55,* 3, 207-218.

Trowbridge, M.H., & Cason, H. (1932). An experimental study of Thorndike's theory of learning. *Journal of General Psychology, 7,* 245-258.

Tsutsui, S., Lee, T.D., & Hodges, N.J. (1998). Contextual interference in learning new patterns of bimanual coordination. *Journal of Motor Behavior, 30,* 2, 151-157.

Ulrich, B.D., & Reeve, T.G. (2005). Studies in motor behavior: 75 years of research in motor development, learning, and control. *Research Quarterly for Exercise and Sport, 76,* 2, S62-S70.

University of Southern California Division of Biokinesiology and Physical Therapy. (n.d.). Carolee J. Winstein, PhD, PT, FAPTA. Retrieved July 6, 2009, from http://pt.usc.edu/SubLayout.aspx?id=366.

University of Southern California Division of Biokinesiology and Physical Therapy. (n.d.). Motor Behavior and Neurorehabilitation Laboratory. Retrieved July 6, 2009, from http://pt.usc.edu/SubLayout.aspx?menu_id=68&id=138&ID&ekmensel=568fab5c_68_70_btnlink&ekmensel=568fab5c_68_70_btnlink.

Vickers, J.N. (1992). Gaze control in putting. *Perception, 21,* 1, 117-132.

Vickers, J.N. (1996). Control of visual attention during the basketball free throw. *American Journal of Sports Medicine, 24,* 6, 93-97.

Vickers, J.N. (1996). Visual control when aiming at a far target. *Journal of Experimental Psychology, 22,* 2, 342-354.

Vickers, J.N. (2007). *Perception, Cognition, and Decision Training: The Quiet Eye in Action.* Champaign, IL: Human Kinetics.

Wade, M.G. (1976). Developmental motor learning. In J. Keogh & R.S. Hutton (Eds.), *Exercise and Sport Sciences Reviews,* Vol. 4. Santa Barbara, CA: Journal Publishing Affiliates.

Wadman, W.J., Denier van der Gon, J.J., Geuze, R.H., & Mol, C.R. (1979). Control of fast goal-directed arm movements. *Journal of Human Movement Studies, 5,* 3-17.

Walter, C. (1998). An alternative view of dynamical systems concepts in motor control and learning. *Research Quarterly for Exercise and Sport, 69,* 4, 326-333.

Ward, P., & Williams, A.M. (2003). Perceptual and cognitive skill development in soccer: The multidimensional nature of expert performance. *Journal of Sport and Exercise Psychology, 25,* 1, 93-111.

Ward, P., Williams, A.M., & Bennett, S.J. (2002). Visual search and biological motion perception in tennis. *Research Quarterly for Exercise and Sport, 73,* 1, 107-112.

Williams, A.M., Singer, R.N., & Frehlich, S.G. (2002). Quiet eye duration, expertise, and task complexity in near and far aiming tasks. *Journal of Motor Behavior, 34,* 2, 197-207.

Worringham, C.J. (1992). Some historical roots of phenomena and methods in motor behavior research. In G.E. Stelmach & J. Requin (Eds.), *Tutorials in Motor Behavior II* (pp. 67-86). Champaign, IL: Human Kinetics.

Wrisberg, C.A., & Liu, Z. (1991). The effect of contextual variety on the practice, retention, and transfer of an applied motor skill. *Research Quarterly for Exercise and Sport, 62,* 4, 406-412.

Wrisberg, C.A., & Mead, B.J. (1983). Developing coincident timing skill in children: A comparison of training methods. *Research Quarterly for Exercise and Sport, 54,* 1, 67-74.

Wrisberg, C.A., & Pein, R.L. (2002). Note on learners' control of the frequency of model presentation during skill acquisition. *Perceptual and Motor Skills, 94,* 3, 792-794.

Wulf, G., Höss, M., & Prinz, W. (1998). Instructions for motor learning: Differential effects of internal versus external focus of attention. *Journal of Motor Behavior, 30,* 2, 169-179.

Wulf, G., McNevin, N.H., Fuchs, T., Ritter, F., & Toole, T. (2000). Attentional focus in complex skill learning. *Research Quarterly for Exercise and Sport, 71,* 3, 229-239.

Wulf, G., Mercer, J., McNevin, N., & Guadagnoli, M.A. (2004). Reciprocal influences of attentional focus on postural and suprapostural task performance. *Journal of Motor Behavior, 36,* 4, 189-199.

Wulf, G., & Schmidt, R.A. (1988). Variability in practice: Facilitation in retention and transfer through schema formation or context effects? *Journal of Motor Behavior, 20,* 2, 133-149.

Wulf, G., & Schmidt, R.A. (1997). Variability of practice and implicit motor learning. *Journal of Experimental Psychology: Learning, Memory, and Cognition, 23,* 4, 987-1006.

Wulf, G., & Shea, C.H. (2002). Principles derived from the study of simple skills do not generalize to complex skill learning. *Psychonomic Bulletin and Review, 9,* 2, 185-211.

Wulf, G., Shea, C.H., & Matschiner, S. (1998). Frequent feedback enhances complex motor skill learning. *Journal of Motor Behavior, 30,* 2, 180-192.

Wulf, G., Shea, C.H., & Whitacre, C.A. (1998). Physical-guidance benefits in learning a complex motor skill. *Journal of Motor Behavior, 30,* 4, 367-380.

Wulf, G., & Toole, T. (1999). Physical assistance devices in complex motor skill learning: Benefits of a self-controlled practice schedule. *Research Quarterly for Exercise and Sport, 70,* 265-272.

Wulf, G., & Weigelt, C. (1997). Instructions about physical principles in learning a complex motor skill: To tell or not to tell. *Research Quarterly for Exercise and Sport, 68,* 4, 362-367.

Young, D.E., Cohen, M.J., & Husak, W.S. (1993). Contextual interference and motor skill acquisition: On the processes that influence retention. *Human Movement Science, 12,* 5, 577-600.

Young, D.E., & Schmidt, R.A. (1992). Augmented kinematic feedback for motor learning. *Journal of Motor Behavior, 24,* 3, 261-273.

Index

Note: The italicized *f* and *t* following page numbers refer to figures and tables, respectively.

About the Author

Jeffrey T. Fairbrother is an associate professor at the University of Tennessee in Knoxville. He teaches graduate and undergraduate courses on motor learning and control and a graduate course on expert performance in sports. His research focuses on the effects that factors related to the performance setting (such as practice schedules) have on the performance and learning of motor skills. He established a collaborative agreement with the U.S. Army Research Institute of Environmental Medicine to investigate the effectiveness of self-controlled feedback on marksmanship training. In addition to his laboratory-based research, his scholarly publications include an article on the forensic analysis of a collapsed portable playpen that killed a child and an article on the take-off maneuver in the sport of surfing. Dr. Fairbrother is an active member of the North American Society for the Psychology of Sport and Physical Activity, and he chaired the Motor Learning/Control Program Committee for their 2006 annual meeting. He also serves as a section editor in motor learning and control for *Research Quarterly for Exercise and Sport*.

Dr. Fairbrother earned a PhD in movement science with a specialization in motor behavior from Florida State University, an MS in physical education from California Polytechnic State University, and a BA in English from the University of California at Santa Barbara.